MARY IMMACULATE COLLEGE

Presented by

**Institiúid Teangeolaíochta Éireann**

2006

# CREATING THE
# LIBRARY IDENTITY
## a manual of design

# CREATING THE LIBRARY IDENTITY
## a manual of design

## JOHN KIRBY

Librarian, Faculty of Art and Design,
Sheffield City Polytechnic, England

Gower A Grafton Book

Published by
Gower Publishing Company Limited,
Gower House,
Croft Road,
Aldershot,
Hants GU11 3HR,
England

and

Gower Publishing Company
Old Post Road,
Brookfield,
Vermont 05036,
U.S.A.

Kirby, John
    Creating the library identity : a manual of
design. — (A Grafton book)
    1. Libraries   2. Industrial design coordination
I. Title
021.7      Z665

ISBN 0-566-03496-4

Printed in Great Britain at the
University Press, Cambridge

# CONTENTS

# Acknowledgements

I would like to thank all those who assisted me directly or indirectly in the writing of this book. In particular I would like to thank Patsy Cullen for her help in formulating my ideas; Mike Holmes who taught me a lot; Tim Cousens for technical assistance; David Lewis, Librarian of Sheffield City Polytechnic, for permission to use material originally developed for the Polytechnic Library; Horst Ernestus for allowing the use of material from Stadtbibliothek Wuppertal; Lesley Machin for typing the manuscript; and my colleagues in the Faculty of Art & Design.

Perhaps the biggest acknowledgement should go to my family, who have lived with the project for the last two years.

## DISCLAIMER

The views expressed in this book are those of the author and not necessarily the views or opinions of Sheffield City Polytechnic Library.

# Introduction

All librarians are concerned with communication and the provision of information and although considerable effort is often put into making this information available to the library's users, too little thought has been given in the past to the environment within which the user is expected to interact with the library.

Too often the library's image is one that is old-fashioned or off-putting so that the user is not encouraged to make the most effective use of the service. Librarians do not deliberately seek to create this effect of course. Perhaps it is merely a lack of thought, or an over-familiarity with the library, which prevents a consideration of the value of creating a positive identity for the library. Just as large numbers of our social and commercial institutions have benefitted from the attention given to their corporate identities and public image, so too should libraries reflect the sophisticated expectations of late twentieth century society. Only in this way can the library continue to be service relevant to the widest community.

This book aims to provide a manual for librarians who have had little or no training in the development of an effective visual environment for the library's users. It provides a basis on which to create an identity for libraries of all sizes and functions.

In addition to the examples in the text there are further illustrations on colour microfiche which show how the ideas explained in the manual have been used in practice. The folder at the end of the book also contains examples of copyright-free artwork which can be used by librarians in their own schemes, either as they stand or with the addition of local data such as addresses, logos etc.

# 1. The Library Identity

Every individual has an image, indeed a number of images, depending on the stance of the viewer. For example, a person may be perceived as lazy, hard-working, efficient, friendly, morose, etc. and everyone with whom he comes in contact will form an impression of him. Such images are often formed initially from the visual appearance of the person and these first impressions tend to persist and be the most significant in forming a relationship. They also seem to be difficult to change at a later date. Since such images exist it would seem sensible to try to create a situation in which they are favourable ones. To some extent this is beyond our control since these perceptions are in the minds of other people, but it is possible to present a specific image of oneself in relationships with others and to mask factors which are detrimental to that image. Thus a librarian could try to hide the seething fury and irritation felt at the sight of a particular reader and present an image of helpful, polite, efficiency!

The same mechanisms operate at an organisational level and many companies spend large amounts on the manipulation of their public image. In part this is done by advertising, but an important element in this process can be the development of a corporate identity. This is the public face of the company and is concerned with a range of activities, the best known of which is probably the concept of a logo or company symbol. This is not necessarily the most important part of the identity programme however, which if carried out properly and to its full conclusion will affect all aspects of the company's processes. The image of a chain of stores for example will be created by the visual appearance of the building, both inside and out, the service provided, staff training, the quality of goods, etc. Such a consciously sought image should be differentiated from the randomly achieved one and the term *identity* is used throughout this book to mean such a deliberately created effect.

Libraries can no longer afford to ignore their image. The image of the library will ultimately influence the availability of funds and resources and the whole future of the institution. A poor image will mean that the library is held in low esteem by its users and consequently it will appear as a service in which there is little point investing money. It is crucial therefore that in any time of financial restraint the library seek to create a positive identity for itself. It is no longer enough to *be* a valuable service; it is now necessary that the

1

library is identified as such so that when discussions of cuts in expenditure take place the library is not seen as an obvious first target.

The creation of specific identities for commercial organisations is probably one that is familiar to all. The evidence of the corporate identity programmes of many major companies can be seen in any high street, yet most people are unaware of the underlying reasons for this effort. The setting-up of a corporate identity programme in a company is an important event, not undertaken lightly. It is usually done for a variety of reasons, often precipitated by some change in the management of the organisation. It is *not* done to make the company prettier, though that may be a side effect; it is *not* done just to keep the design department in work, nor is it the simple whim of the managing director. The corporate identity programme should weld together the component parts of the organisation, provide an easily recognisable appearance for the organisation, provide a rational and consistent approach to the organisation's activities, and by all of these produce some improvement in the organisation's performance. But whatever the reasons that are given for the introduction of the programme the underlying motive is that which drives every commercial organisation — profit. The benefits of the corporate identity programme will be various, often difficult to identify or to ascribe for certain to the programme itself, but the overall result will be one that produces some positive benefit for the company. Anyone who has any doubts about the importance of the profit factor in such an activity should be aware that most major chain stores can tell the profitability not just of each of their stores, or even of departments within each store, but the costs and profit margins of every square metre that they own.

Concern with profit is uppermost, and money will not be expended which does not give at least some hope of a return. The development of a corporate identity programme is important to many commercial organisations and libraries should take this into account, since although libraries are not directly seeking profits, they should be seeking the effective use of resources.

Libraries are concerned with processes which have analogies in commercial organisations. It is useful to consider how companies tackle problems and to learn from these. The counterpart activities are not completely analogous (it is unlikely that they could be since libraries are rather unusual institutions), but there are similarities of operation.

## MANY LIBRARY SYSTEMS ARE DISPERSED, WITH SERVICE POINTS IN A VARIETY OF BUILDINGS AND LOCATIONS.

An organisation with similar features on a much larger scale is a railway system, with a multitude of stations, of varying sizes and appearance. Most railways of the world have adopted a clear corporate identity programme following the lead of British Rail. The most disparate railway stations are linked by the use of a logo, common lettering for signs and names. Other elements of the service bear the same features. Thus British Rail's road vehicles are identified by the same logo and lettering, as are engines, rolling stock, staff uniforms and stationery.

Why do railways make this effort? Obviously it is in their interest to advertise their services, but it could be argued that railway stations are not difficult buildings to find once you are in the immediate vicinity. The answer lies in the desire to provide a coordinated and instantly recognisable visual message. Society is full of visual stimuli and each one of us is constantly being overburdened to the extent that the brain automatically screens out a high proportion of the potential images. An example of this can be seen when driving a car. The brain ignores (or should ignore) the minute detail of the streets, the buildings, the shops. Instead it picks out road signs, potential hazards, other traffic. At times it will pick out other detail, but this too is usually something of interest to the driver, a familiar-looking face, another car of the same make as his. If the screening process did not take place we would be overwhelmed by the data from the visual information presented to us. The brain selects those items which are relevant to present thoughts or activities. Thus when we are looking for the station the brain already knows what it is looking for. The visual appearance of the railway station provides a clear unambiguous message. The impact of the logo and typeface is effective because they fit a pattern which is familiar from having been seen at *other* railway stations. The brain likes familiar patterns and identifies these faster than unfamiliar ones. If the stations were all labelled differently they would be harder to find. Similar use of logos and standardised signs can be seen on banks, post offices, building societies, chain stores etc. Because of the previous experience of the sign it becomes an easily read code. Compare the familiarity of the known environment with the innate 'strangeness' found when visiting foreign countries, where the patterns are different and unfamiliar.

Libraries too ought to be concerned with being recognisable in the same way, with branches being seen as part of a larger system. Librarians like to boast that even the smallest service point can provide the most esoteric book through being part of a larger network, but many users, not unnaturally, expect far less from a small branch than a central library. One way of countering this is to provide a visual link between the libraries in the system, proclaiming that they belong together.

## LIBRARIES ARE CONCERNED WITH PROVIDING BITS OF INFORMATION TO THEIR USERS, PREDOMINANTLY IN THE FORM OF A DOCUMENT SUCH AS A BOOK, JOURNAL, VIDEO, MICROFICHE, ETC.

For most library users this is a self-service process; they go to the shelves and select the item they need. For those who cannot find what they want librarians are available to assist. This in essence appears to be what most libraries are about for most of their users.

# biscuits ↘

**Fish Market** ↗
**Meat Market** →
← **Exit: New Square**
↙ **Toilets**

*Guiding in stores is frequently better than in libraries*

An analogous organisation would be a large store which is concerned with directing its customers to the appropriate part of the building where they can make a selection from the goods available. Staff are usually on hand to answer queries. No shop of any size however expects its customers to wander round with no guidance. If the customer in the department store is seeking carpets it is no good expecting him to start in the basement and walk up and down the stairs until he finds them. Some form of guiding or signposting is usually provided, and this has to be of a sufficiently effective standard to ensure that the public can find most of what they want without resorting to the staff for help. The store expects only a very small minority of its customers to need such assistance. Providing a member of staff to tell every customer where to find the dog food, cosmetics or car accessories would be an expensive solution to the problem of guiding the store. Signs are far cheaper. For guiding to be most effective it needs to be part of a coordinated system and this too is part of the corporate identity programme. All the signs should have a relationship to each other, in typeface, size, positioning, colour etc so that their message will be clear and easily understood. The rationale to guiding the interior of the building is similar to that of its outside.

Few libraries provide guiding as efficient as their nearest big supermarket, yet the number of items held by even large hypermarkets is small compared with the number of books in even a modest library service point. Librarians are compelled to waste valuable time, not on "genuine" enquiries, but on simple directional queries such as

"Where are the toilets?"
"Where are the books on gardening?"
"Where is 658?"
"Where do I go to find the newspapers?"

Obviously the effectiveness of the library could be improved both for the users and the staff by using the techniques employed in the store.

## LIBRARIES ARE ORGANISATIONS DEPENDENT ON THEIR USERS FOR MONEY.

In some countries such as Holland this may take the form of a subscription to join the library but in most cases the source of library revenue will be less direct, through a local authority, educational institution etc. These resources are usually controlled by elected representatives from the community. Indirectly therefore the library is funded by the people who use it, and those who don't use it. Analogous organisations relying on money from their customers are banks and building societies who seek to attract funds from people by providing interest, or a service such as a cheque book. If the organisation is rude or inefficient its customers are likely to take their money elsewhere. Banks and building societies therefore try to build up a relationship with their customers by providing efficient services, offering advice or help with financial problems and in particular by showing a friendly face to their users, even attempting to humanise the bank manager's image in their advertising. Their overall message is that they care about each one of their customers as an individual despite the intense mechanisation of their operations. The library too ought to use some of these ploys to create a positive identity among its users, as it should be remembered that the library users ultimately pay for the library and its services and there is a positive benefit to be gained from *not* antagonising them unnecessarily. Staff can be trained to adopt a friendly tone when talking to users, and can appear approachable when at the enquiry desk. The use of badges or nameplates on desks to identify staff as individuals can give the impression at least that they are human beings too. In addition to communication to those ultimately providing the finance the library needs to pay particular attention to those who make the decisions about the library. These could be local councillors, members of senate in a university, deans of faculties, etc. The librarian must identify these key people and ensure that they are provided with a clear picture of the library and its needs. Libraries need all the support they can get; there are enough negative images already through apathy without deliberately creating more.

## LIBRARIES ARE FREQUENTLY MADE UP OF DISPARATE PARTS.

This may be due to the merger of institutions or authorities, where staff suddenly find themselves with new allegiances and working with new colleagues. Often however it is simply caused by functional or geographical divisions in the library. The staff in the cataloguing department may keep themselves to themselves, or the librarians in the art library may feel that they have little in common with the law librarians across the campus. Similar situations are commonplace in industry and business, either due to mergers, takeovers or because of the size of the organisations.

The corporate identity programme can be used to provide separate areas of the company with an overall identity which transcends their own particular subdivision. The use of standardised stationery, newsletters, logos, house style for publications, livery for vehicles, all provide a reminder to staff of the framework in which they work.

It is important that the library staff have a clear idea of the library's identity and can see the wider context of their own activities. Without this guidance they may be working at odds with each other and have different priorities from the main aims and objectives of the library.

The corporate identity programme cannot be developed without a clear knowledge of these objectives and the means by which they are to be achieved, but once the programme is operating it is itself a vehicle for the dissemination of these aims throughout the organisation.

For the librarian seeking to improve his library's identity these are the main points to consider:

# Target audiences for
# Library Communications

1. The community in which the Library is set.

2. Users of the Library.

3. Providers of resources.

4. Library staff.

*5. _ _ _ _ _ _ _ _ _ _ _ _ _ _ _ _ _ _ _

6. _ _ _ _ _ _ _ _ _ _ _ _ _ _ _ _ _ _ _

7. _ _ _ _ _ _ _ _ _ _ _ _ _ _ _ _ _ _ _

8. _ _ _ _ _ _ _ _ _ _ _ _ _ _ _ _ _ _ _

9. _ _ _ _ _ _ _ _ _ _ _ _ _ _ _ _ _ _ _

10. _ _ _ _ _ _ _ _ _ _ _ _ _ _ _ _ _ _

*Add your specific targets here

1 The appearance of the library in the community and its recognisability to users and non-users.
2 Communication with users inside the service point, in terms of guiding, signposting, staff activity etc.
3 Communication to those who provide resources.
4 Communication to the library staff about the organisation, its objectives and their place in its structure.

By paying attention to the identity of the library it should be possible to affect each of these audiences. The corporate identity programme is not something that is an afterthought that can be considered if there is any time or money left at the end of the day. It should be an integral part of the library's planning and should be given the resources to achieve its ends. The effective communication by the library to the audiences listed above is as central to the library's activities as producing an efficient catalogue or manning an effective information desk, but it is an area of activity which has been grossly neglected in the past. If libraries are to be of any relevance in the future however it is necessary to give some form of identity programme the attention it has previously lacked. Without it the library risks losing out on resources as the competition for funds increases.

# 2. Setting-up the Identity Programme

The advantages of the corporate identity approach to the library's communication with its various publics are considerable, but the design and implementation of the programme is not an easy task. The first need is for the acceptance of the value of the programme by senior staff in the library. Without this approval the identity programme has little chance of success. Responsibility for the implementation of the programme should be given to a senior librarian, even if much of the actual work on the scheme is done by more junior staff. It is certain that the identity programme will engender change in the appearance of the library, possibly changes in working practices and even changes in the way that the library staff are expected to act towards the public. Only the authority of a senior member of the library staff can ensure that these changes actually take place. Many libraries leave the responsibility for guiding etc to junior staff who then have to spend a lot of time negotiating with senior colleagues to get things done and changes introduced. The actual work of the programme can usually be handed over to a junior librarian provided that the ultimate responsibility and authority is clearly laid down and apparent to the rest of the staff.

## THE LIBRARIAN AND THE GRAPHIC DESIGNER

It is a fortunate library which can employ the services of a full-time graphic designer on its staff. This is an ideal situation since the designer is the expert in this field and will be able to produce far better results than can be achieved by amateurs. Unfortunately many libraries are too small to justify such a post, or the librarians feel that the needs of the basic library service mean that every effort has to be put into services more directly related to the needs of the readers.

Where a graphic designer is used the librarian responsible for the programme should ensure that the work is divided appropriately. Most importantly the designer should be given a clear brief for each part of the programme. This requires that the librarian is himself clear what he is trying to achieve, and this thought and analysis is itself an important part in the development of the scheme.

# BALANCE OF RESPONSIBILITIES

The following are guidelines on how the work should be split between the librarian and designer:

the librarian should
1 Identify needs
2 Coordinate the programme
3 Analyse information
4 Consider format and presentation
5 Decide quantities
6 Oversee expenditure
7 Ensure that library staff carry out the programme correctly
8 Act as an interface between the library and the designer.

The designer should
1 Prepare costings
2 Decide format
3 Design and prepare artwork, signs, etc
4 Arrange typing, typesetting, etc
5 Arrange printing and liaise with printer
6 Spend the budget on materials and printing.

These divisions are not of course hard and fast but are open to a certain amount of negotiation between the participants. Certain points are fixed however. The final decision in any matter should be the librarian's, though he should always bear in mind the expertise of the designer and should not ignore his advice without reason. Only *one* person should liaise with the printers and other professionals, such as photographers, who are involved in the implementation of the programme. Printers in particular should not be harassed by librarians who have nothing to do with the production of materials. It will not help for a branch librarian to ring the printers in a temper because he is waiting for some particular stationery. All such chasing should be done through one person. Similarly the printer needs to be able to contact one person in the library to deal with any problems arising from his end and it is probably best if this person is the designer. The librarian in the team should be responsible for ensuring that all text is appropriate. The level of such editing powers needs to be worked out at the initial stages of implementation. Since it is likely that he will be relying on his colleagues to provide much of this text he must be capable of persuading them if certain parts much be changed. In particular he should look out for the use of library jargon. Librarians, like other specialists, often forget that they use a specialised language, not easily understandable to non-librarians. It can be salutary to show draft texts to people who have little experience of libraries and see if they understand them. The designer himself may be a useful such guinea pig.

The new MICROFICHE CATALOGUE is in two parts.

# 1. AUTHOR-TITLE CATALOGUE

Use this part if you know an author's name, the title of a book or an artist's name.

# 2. SUBJECT

Use this part to find what books are in the Library on a particular topic.

If the subject you are interested in is a person you should also look in the Author-Title Catalogue as there may be entries there too that will be of use.

When you find the item you want in the catalogue, it will look something like this:

PERLMAN, Bernard B.
The Immortal Eight;  American Paintings from
Eakins to the Armoury Show, 1870-1913/by
Bernard B. Perlman.
North Light, 1979.
224p.
   (Ashcan School/Painting, American - 19th century/PL
   0/0891340173/Title number A8000082)
       PSALTER LANE ←
       Copies 01
       Subject number AXC PE          This indicates that
                                      there is a copy at
                                      Psalter Lane

                                      You will find the book
                                      on the shelf at this
                                      classmark.

If the book is not on the shelves, you can reserve it at the Library Counter.

Please ask a member of the Library Staff for help in using the catalogue if you have any queries or if you cannot find what you are looking for.

*Jargon can be avoided*

# WITHOUT THE GRAPHIC DESIGNER

Where the library cannot employ its own designer however there is no need to abandon the concept of the identity programme. Most libraries are part of larger institutions or organisations. Often these larger bodies will employ a designer and the librarian should try to make use of him. If this does not meet with success it may be necessary to call in a specialist consultant to help set up the programme in such a way that it can be carried out within the library's own structure. The final solution is for the librarian to take on a dual role. This is particularly difficult. The librarian who has taken on the task of carrying through the programme may lack the technical skill of producing artwork etc. The other major problem is that he is unlikely to have enough time to devote to the programme, since this will often be merely one job amongst his many duties and it is quite likely that it will only be seen as a minor duty compared to the bulk of his job description. The technical inadequcy can be overcome in most cases; much can be learnt, painfully, by trial and error; even more can be gained by going on a short course or working with an experienced designer.

Whether the librarian is using an outside designer or is going to do the job himself it is essential that a brief is drawn up so that everyone is clear about the job in hand. This should include details of the audience, budgetary restraints, timescale etc. Even if the librarian is working on his own he will probably still need some technical support to help with artwork, the construction of guiding etc. The main requirement is to avoid the amateurish appearance associated with wobbly lettering, wrong spacing and poor layout. The necessary skills for this work can usually be found in the library though may not be immediately obvious. Look out for someone with art school training perhaps or a qualification in technical drawing. Alternatively send someone on a short course, or look outside the library for this back-up. On the whole qualified librarians are not very skilled in this field. If proof of this is needed look at the guiding and publications in most libraries.

If all other sources fail it is possible to go out to printers or copyshops, many of which will do the artwork as well as the printing job.

This may appear expensive but the final results will be presentable at the very least and the costs should be balanced against the hidden costs of production within the library and the quality of the final work.

# INTRODUCING THE IDENTITY PROGRAMME

The introduction of the identity programme should be carefully explained to all staff. Most will probably welcome it on the whole. It is important to stress the positive improvements that will result from the programme, improved guiding, easier to use forms, economies of production, rather than to attempt initially to provide a theoretical rationale for its introduction. The underlying concepts can be introduced later. Beware of using jargon terms like *corporate identity* when explaining the programme to the staff, particularly junior staff, and even more particularly if the explanation is to a large group where feedback from individuals is not easy to monitor. The words *corporate identity*, like the phrase *Aims and Objectives*, have negative connotations in many minds, due to their occasional use in commerce to impose management ideas in an insensitive manner. Any serious doubts that are expressed by staff should be discussed in depth and decisions taken on which course to follow. Despite the best endeavours of the identity programme and its creators it is possible for even the most junior member of staff to sabotage all its intentions by wilful disobedience or negative attitudes caused through ignorance. It will fail in its purpose if staff are rude to the readers, or are lazy or careless in their work. Consider the state of some of the nationalised industries which all have highly developed corporate identity programmes, but not always the staff to live up to the corporately desired approach. The best guiding in the world will be of little avail in creating the library identity if the library assistant stamping out books spends his time chatting to his friend while he deals with the readers. It is best therefore if the staff can be relied on to follow the ideas laid down in the identity programme and not to undermine these efforts. In order for this to be achieved they need to be kept informed.

## RESOURCING THE PROGRAMME

It is not possible to run the identity programme without a budget. It is not expected that the library will spend the proportion of its gross revenue that is spent by industry or commerce on developing their identities but as always the library will get what it pays for. If a guiding system is needed, and it is in most libraries, then money must be made available to buy materials; if the library wants a publications programme then it must be prepared to pay for printing. It should be possible to show some economies, particularly on stationery production where there are usually duplication and inefficiencies that can be eradicated, but the main benefits of the programme will be difficult if not impossible to assess in monetary terms. One German librarian has said that he could see a correlation between the amount he spent on his identity programme and the success of his library in terms of usage and consequently in an increased budget. Analysis of library use however is an area fraught with problems, and probably all that can be said is that if the library emulates industry and commerce in its approach to corporate identity then it will reap many of the same benefits that these sectors gain from the activity.

In addition to money adequate staff resources must be provided to carry out the programme. It is difficult to see how any librarian can do all this work in odd moments, though clearly there are librarians who have made time amongst their other work and have achieved success at it. If technician or library assistant help is available however it is essential that there are clear guidelines on the amount of time these staff will spend on the programme. Without such agreements there are too many areas of potential conflict between their immediate supervisors and the librarian responsible for the identity programme.

## ANALYSIS AND DESIGN OF THE PROGRAMME

After these problems have all been sorted out the design of the programme itself can begin. The first step is the analysis of the overall aims and objectives of the library. In some organisations this is in the form of a published statement but in many libraries they are vague assumptions and generalisations. If this is the case it is necessary to draw up some broad written objectives which should be agreed by at least the senior management team in the library. The aims of the corporate identity programme should now be drawn up and matched against this list to ensure that the two are in harmony. For example if one of the policies of the library is to provide only a closed access service to its readers there is little point in the identity programme providing a detailed guiding system aimed at the public. Alternatively if the library is attempting to reduce the amount of time spent by professional staff on unproductive low-level enquiry work then the introduction of such a guiding scheme would seem to be highly compatible with that aim.

Examples of existing stationery, publications etc should be collected together and an assessment made of what will be needed, what can be amalgamated and what must be replaced with something new. It is a salutary experience at this stage to pin all these pieces of paper to a board or wall, along with photographs of service points and vehicles and look at them en masse. If there is any corporate identity already in existence it should be possible to see it. If it does exist it may be worth building on what is there already. In most libraries however they merely look like a random collection of bits of paper.

Decisions need to be taken on the overall design of the identity programme, and the design of some of the key elements should be tried to test the decisions on typefaces, logo, formats etc. It is a good idea to make mock-ups of some items of stationery, guiding and publications or better still to experiment in one service point rather than suddenly jump in with a complete scheme for the whole library system. If the trials are successful then a timetable should be drawn up for the introduction of the identity programme in full. Not that such a timetable will necessarily be adhered to slavishly. Problems may well arise which necessitate a rethink, or it may simply take much longer than was expected to implement the guiding systems in a big library. The timetable does provide a useful reference point against which to measure the scheme, and this should be rewritten as appropriate at regular intervals. Librarians familiar with an aims and objectives approach to library management will be used to this process.

# THE IDENTITY MANUAL

The elements of the identity programme should now be drawn up in the form of a manual to ensure their consistent use. This manual should be referred to before any part of the programme is implemented. The manual should deal with the following main subject areas:

## 1  LOGO

The logo is the standardised form of the library's name. It is one of the key elements in providing the recognisability of the library. It may involve a symbol or the use of a particular typeface, or both. It is most important that the logo is used in a consistent manner. The manual should lay down instructions for its use, including size of type, layout, position, colours etc. The inconsistent use of the logo defeats its whole purpose which is to provide an easily recognisable form of the library's name. Unless there is a relevant symbol already in use in the organisation it is probably better to avoid the use of such non-verbal designs. Because of their abstract nature it is often difficult to know what the symbol is intended to mean. A meaning clear to librarians may be totally obscure to others. It is better to stick to type alone to create the library logo.

## 2  TYPEFACES

The manual should indicate what typeface should be used in a variety of situations in order to ensure consistency. There will probably be a need for one typeface for guiding which may be different from those used in stationery, publications, etc.

## 3  COLOURS

The manual should state which colours are to be used and for what purpose. If possible samples of paper, card, inks should be included so that these are quite clear. A statement for example that the library's signs will always be blue is not precise enough since there are so many possible variant blue colours.

## 4  FORMATS, SIZE, LAYOUT

The manual should indicate a range of formats for various categories of publications, stationery, guiding and examples of layout should be provided.

**WESTBRIDGE**
**UNIVERSITY**
# LIBRARY

*Logo*

**WESTBRIDGE**
**UNIVERSITY**
## LIBRARY
### PSALTER LANE SITE

*Logo plus Site Name*

**WESTBRIDGE**
**UNIVERSITY**
## LIBRARY
PSALTER LANE SITE
Psalter Lane

*Logo plus Site Name & Address*

*The Library Logo*

**WESTBRIDGE
UNIVERSITY
LIBRARY**    1982·83    PL
CC
WW

This card must be produced each time
a book is borrowed.

Loss of this card must be reported to
the Library immediately.

Signature

---

**WESTBRIDGE
UNIVERSITY
LIBRARY**
PSALTER LANE SITE
Psalter Lane

Telephone
56101
Ext. 30

Please see no.

1. Please extend the loan period. At present
   it is due back on

2. The loan period has now been extended. It
   is now due back on

*This Logo should usually be in the top left corner*

| | |
|---|---|
| Mr Ms Dr<br>Mrs Miss   Surname | **WESTBRIDGE<br>UNIVERSITY<br>LIBRARY** |
| Forenames | **Enrolment form** |
| Termtime<br>Address | Please tick:<br>  Full time student<br>  Part time student<br>  Staff<br>  Other |
| Home Address<br>(if different) | Please circle<br>year of course |
| Course      Department | 1  2  3  4  5 |
| Details of employer if<br>short course/conference member | For Library Staff use |
| Signature      Date | |

| | |
|---|---|
| Author   (Block Capitals) | Reader's surname & initials |
| Title | |
| Class | Book/Copy number |
| Date borrowed | Date due |
| **WESTBRIDGE<br>UNIVERSITY<br>LIBRARY**    Issue Slip | Reader's signature |

*In some cases it is necessary to choose an
alternative place to put the logo
Here the usual place is needed for filing words*

# 5 METHODS OF PRODUCTION

Where possible methods of production should be stipulated, though there is likely to be more room for flexibility here depending on what is available. For example "if more than 20 copies are required use the Print Unit, if less than 20 use the xerox machine unless this produces unacceptable copies". It should also specify the use of particular dry lettering systems, or the use of lettering machines, stencils, etc.

The implementation of the identity programme in each library is highly individual to each system but the following points should be considered:

1 Responsibility to the programme should rest with a senior librarian.
2 There should be the involvement of a designer or design consultant at an early stage of the implementation of the scheme.
3 The reasons for the programme should be explained to all staff.
4 There should be an adequate budget set aside for the programme.
5 There must be adequate staff time made available, particularly of any junior staff or technicians involved in the programme.
6 The aims and objectives of the library must be considered and the aims of the identity programme matched to these.
7 The existing stationery etc should be examined and evaluated.
8 A design manual should be produced to ensure consistency in the introduction of the programme.

With these guidelines in mind the librarian can now begin to think about the technical and practical aspects of the programme.

# 3.  Tools and Equipment

The tools and equipment that the librarian who is concerned with the identity programme will need vary depending on how much he can rely on other skilled staff. If he is able to use the services of a graphic designer he obviously needs few tools himself. A catalogue of dry transfer lettering on his bookshelf, or better still a chart on his wall will make his office look 'arty', as will a noticeboard on which he can pin examples of the programme's output! The librarian who has to do more than just liaise with a designer however needs to acquire a basic set of tools in order to do straightforward artwork, hang signs and guiding, etc. This equipment need not be expensive and most needs will be met by the items on the Shopping List and Tool Box (pp 22 and 25).

## EQUIPMENT FOR ARTWORK

The first essential is somewhere flat to work on. A drawing board is the ideal, but a flat piece of melamine or similar board will do just as well. There is no need to buy an expensive drawing table costing hundreds of pounds. Most of the artwork needed for the implementation of the programme will be A4 or A3 size so a drawing board which is A2 size, about 42 x 60 cm, is plenty big enough. This size has the added advantage that it is easily portable.

The drawing board will probably have a moving arm enabling you to draw horizontal lines. If using a home-made board a T-square will be necessary. Since vertical lines are needed a large set-square should also be purchased. Some of the more expensive drawing boards include this.

The next essentials are a ruler, pencils and a soft eraser. Some form of pens are also needed but do not buy tools you cannot use. Unless you are a competent artist it is not really worth getting top quality drawing pens. For most of the artwork a variety of black fibre pens in different widths will be adequate. These can be used for filling holes in rub-down lettering, line drawings, adding straight lines etc.

Lettering for headings on stationery and publications will probably be done with dry transfer lettering. It is useful to keep an old ball-pen for rubbing down the letters. It is possible to get special burnishers for this but completely unnecessary; the pen works just as well. Text of publications will be produced on an electric typewriter, a compositor

# SHOPPING LIST

Drawing Board
Set & T-Squares
Ruler
Pens & Pencils
Masking Tape
Glue
Scissors, Scalpel
Tweezers
Eraser

or on a word processor. Each can provide good results; the choice will probably depend on what the librarian has access to. If headings need to be centred on the page it is worth investing in a little kit which allows you to lay down the lettering as complete words rather than as individual letters. One company markets a Word Positioning System which can save a lot of the frustration arising from words which are not quite centred. Alternatively put the words onto a separate piece of paper and paste-up in the correct place. Even easier is not to centre anything but to line everything up on a left-hand margin.

Masking tape is another essential buy; use it to stick down the corners of the paper on the drawing board; also to lift off lettering that needs removing. Since most artwork will be made using the paste-up technique some form of glue is necessary. Spray glue is the best since it is applied in an even film and also allows the paper to be lifted off again and repositioned. Beware however — do not get spray glue on the artwork itself, or on your fingers. It is all too easy for dust to stick to the glue and form dirty marks which are not removeable without a lot of effort. Spray glue and aerosols of any kind should only be used in a well-ventilated environment. Paste-up also requires some form of cutting tool. Scissors or a stanley knife can be used, but a scalpel is an even more useful thing to have on hand. It can be used to cut out small pieces and with some practice it is possible to excise wrong words or even individual letters from the text and replace them with the correct ones. Larger cutting jobs need a hand guillotine or trimmer. A pair of tweezers aids the paste-up process considerably and removes the need to put smudgy fingerprints on the artwork when handling very small pieces of paper. Once the paste-up job is complete unwanted lines and marks can be removed with a soft eraser, painted over with typewriter erasing fluid, or in desperate circumstances covered with a layer of white paper.

## MORE ADVANCED EQUIPMENT

The above basic kit will allow the production of artwork for many straight-forward jobs, but if illustrations are to be included the equipment must be extended. There is no need to buy these machines however since their use will be relatively limited, but you need to have access to:

A camera to take black and white prints of illustrations. Note that they can then be altered in size in the printing process or even reversed, made into negative copies etc. Alternatively pictures can be traced and turned into line drawings using a black pen. Unfortunately it is not always possible to find a picture the correct size for tracing. A simple solution is to use an epidiascope which will project an image of the picture, or even a three-dimensional object, onto a screen. Pin a piece of white paper to the wall and adjust the size of the image until it is the correct size on this sheet. Then draw round the projected image in pencil. Finish it off by drawing in the outlined main features with a black pen. The gangsters poster on page 58 was produced in this way:

It requires absolutely no artistic skill to achieve an acceptable result. There are often sophisticated enlargers available in graphic design studios but the epidiascope works just as well!

Once the artwork has been completed it is necessary to keep it clean. The professional sticks it onto stiff board and covers it with thin paper. Alternatively place it in a clear plastic wallet and store in flat cardboard boxes. The sort that x-ray film comes in are very useful. They can usually be obtained from the nearest hospital x-ray department free if you talk nicely to the staff there.

## TOOLS FOR GUIDING

A basic toolkit will be needed for the erection of signs and guiding in the library. The actual construction of plastic and wood signs will possibly be done by commercial signmakers. If not they require only simple tools and strong glue. The following should provide for most eventualities: small saw; hammer; electric drill and assorted bits, including at least one to cut into masonry; wall-plugs, screws, nails and pins of various sizes; steel tape-measure; screwdrivers (one conventional, one 'posidrive'); small spirit level (there will be plenty of people to tell you that a sign is not straight — avoid the hassle by getting it right first time); fishing line for hanging signs from the ceiling; double-sided tape; sticky pads; glue; and anti-static polish to clean finger marks etc off perspex signs.

Keep these together in a box or carrying case. There is nothing more irritating than to go to hang guiding and find that you have left behind the tape measure or other vital piece of equipment. An old briefcase makes an ideal tool box for this stuff.

One item of equipment which is very useful, though may be too expensive for a small library to buy is a lettering machine. The best ones punch out plastic letters which can then be stuck onto a card or plastic background. Look around the institution or neighbouring institutions if the library cannot afford to buy its own. If there is only a limited amount of work for the machine to do, it may be worth hiring it for a week to get all the lettering prepared for the guiding part of the programme. In a large library system however it is worth making the capital investment to acquire such a machine. It will save hundreds of pounds in dry transfer lettering if there is a lot of guiding to be done. Once the machine is readily available there is a tendency to find it many more jobs to do. The library could even hire it out to other departments or to other libraries!

There are also machines which will laminate small notices with plastic film. It is not necessary to buy one of these unless the library has spare money or can justify the purchase by showing that there is a lot of use for the machine in addition to the work on the identity programme. It is more economical to buy adhesive plastic film by the roll and to find a member of staff with a steady hand and some degree of manual dexterity who can apply the sticky film without too many wrinkles and bubbles.

Saw
Hammer
Screwdrivers
Drill
Tape Measure
Spirit Level
Nails, Pins, Screws
Fishing Line
Glue
Polish
Tape

The cost of both the "shopping list" and "toolbox" is quite low and their contents represent a minimum of equipment to achieve a successful identity programme. Obviously individual librarians will want to add to the list as experience exposes the need. Beware however, graphic design shops can exercise a particular fascination and it is possible to come home with all sorts of gadgets which are so specialised that they will be used only very occasionally or never at all. Consider the analogy of the kitchen shop where you can buy a vast range of tools such as cherry stone removers, garlic shredders etc, all of which are unnecessary in most people's everyday cookery. The contents of the graphics shop or stationer's are very interesting, might be useful, will make your office look like a design studio perhaps, but do not necessarily make your artwork any better. Indulge yourself if you wish, but you do not need to, the identity programme can be realised with a minimum of tools and equipment.

# 4.  Materials and Processes

The librarian responsible for the identity programme must make himself familiar with a wide range of materials and processes and the advantages and disadvantages of each. He must also be aware of what can be achieved within the institution and what must be put out to commercial companies. For example the library might have access to an offset litho machine but with a limited paper size of A4. If the librarian wishes to print an A3 size poster he must therefore go to another printer, perhaps entailing extra costs.

He should be endowed with a resourceful mind, continually on the look out for ways of overcoming particular problems at low cost but with a high quality of the finished product.

## PAPER AND CARD

The most obvious materials that will be used in the identity programme are paper and card. Leaflets, publications, stationery will all be on this. It is important to be critical about the quality of paper for each job. Do not accept the same for each item necessarily, but ask to see samples of alternative paper weights with costs. Ephemeral stationery can be printed on lower grade paper than more prestigous publications. For example the issue slips for an academic library's manual issue system should not be printed on high quality paper but on the flimsiest possible consistent with reasonable opaqueness. The library will probably use thousands of these each week and most of them will have a useful life of only a few weeks before being thrown away after the book itself is discharged. Often these issue slips will be multipart using NCR paper which is quite expensive. Reduce costs as far as possible by lowering the paper quality to a minimum therefore. The librarian's annual report on the other hand should be printed on reasonably good paper, with little show-through of print from one side of the page to the other. Most stationery will fall between these two extremes. But always consider the standard of paper to be used and do not use a higher quality than is necessary. Coloured paper and card normally cost much the same as white so do not shrink from using colours. It is essential to check with the printer however to see that he is not having to buy in coloured stock especially for your small job as this could raise the cost unless he can be certain that you will be using

| | |
|---|---|
| Author (Block Capitals) | Reader's surname & initials |
| Title | |
| Class | Book/Copy number |
| Date borrowed | Date due |
| **WESTBRIDGE UNIVERSITY LIBRARY**   Issue Slip | Reader's signature |

*Produce ephemeral stationery on flimsy paper*

large quantities in the future. It is better to ask to see the colours the printer has available and to choose from these. As with paper so also with card. Card can come in a variety of thicknesses and the costs rise dramatically as thicker card is used. Most of this printing onto paper and card will be in black ink. Coloured inks are available of course and cost no more than black but the use of coloured inks can cause delays in the printing as the machines have to be completely cleaned before the ink colour can be changed. The printer may be reluctant to do this for a small job and so may put the coloured ink job to the bottom of the pile. If using coloured ink therefore check with the printer exactly when it will be ready. Other factors affecting cost include the size of the job and the number of copies to be printed. Note that the unit cost will drop as more copies are printed. Avoid short runs if possible. If the artwork is the wrong size and has to be altered to fit or if the printed sheets have to be cut to size, these will add to the price. If the production is being done within the institution many of these costs may be 'lost' but they are still there, somewhere.

## PRODUCING ARTWORK

When producing printed items it is necessary first to produce an original. This is called artwork and should be in black and white irrespective of what colour the final printing will be. If more than one colour is to printed onto the same sheet then one piece of artwork needs to be made for each colour.

Artwork will also be needed if a photocopier is to be used, and here even more care needs to be taken to ensure that there are no blemishes. Most artwork is now produced by sticking pieces of text, line illustrations, logo etc onto a backing sheet. If this is done with spray adhesive the pieces can be lifted off again and repositioned if necessary. Any marks or blemishes can be painted white with typewriter correcting fluid or covered with white paper. Provided that the artwork is black and white only, all will be well. It does not matter if the edges of the paper pieces show as these will disappear at the next stage. When the artwork is completed and clean put it in a safe place so that it does not get marks on it since any smudges will show on the printed result. The printer will now make a plate from the artwork and print from this. If a photocopier is to be used to run off a small number in the library the artwork must be made up slightly differently. The problem with using the paste up method described above is that the edges of the paper will often be picked up by the machine and appear as black lines. One solution to this is to copy the artwork, then paint out any extra lines with typewriter correcting fluid, and then copy the corrected artwork. This loses some quality however because it is then a copy of a copy, but may be acceptable, depending how good the machine is. Do not forget that coloured paper can be used in such machines with very good results. Because most people's expectations of these copiers is that they operate on white paper the result on coloured paper looks better through being unexpected. Also the

# parliamentary publications

1983

*Paste-up the separate parts forming the Artwork*

**WESTBRIDGE UNIVERSITY LIBRARY**

# parliamentary publications

1983

## Acts

If a bill survives each stage of parliamentary scrutiny, it receives the Royal Assent, and becomes an Act. We receive copies a few days later. Arrangement is by calendar year (rather than session), then by chapter number (a chapter number is a number given to each act published in a certain year).

## House of Lords papers & bills

These are in a single sequence, consisting mainly of bills that originate in the Lords, and of Lords amendments to Commons bills, but it also contains reports of House of Lords committees. They are arranged by session, then document number.

## Command papers

Command papers originate outside Westminster, usually in a government department, and are used to present information and statements on government policy to parliament. The important official documents that are mentioned on TV and in the press are often Command papers: white papers, discussion papers, reports of Committees and Royal Commissions, and so on. They also include the annual reports of certain government bodies, and some statistics. Arrangement is by "Cmnd." number in a single sequence, regardless of the session in which the document appears.

## Hansard

This is a verbatim record of the proceedings of both Houses. We file the issues for the previous 12 months in the Collection, but earlier copies are available back to November 1940, although there are gaps. Ask at the Information Desk if you want any of these. Hansards are arranged in date order.

**Written by Grahame Wills**
**Senior Assistant Subject Librarian, Pond Street Site**

Pond Street Site

**WESTBRIDGE UNIVERSITY LIBRARY** 1982·83 PL CC WW

This card must be produced each time a book is borrowed.

Loss of this card must be reported to the Library immediately.

Signature

**WESTBRIDGE UNIVERSITY LIBRARY** 1982·83 PL CC WW

This card must be produced each time a book is borrowed.

Loss of this card must be reported to the Library immediately.

Signature

**WESTBRIDGE UNIVERSITY LIBRARY** 1982·83 PL CC WW

This card must be produced each time a book is borrowed.

Loss of this card must be reported to the Library immediately.

Signature

**WESTBRIDGE UNIVERSITY LIBRARY** 1982·83 PL CC WW

This card must be produced each time a book is borrowed.

Loss of this card must be reported to the Library immediately.

Signature

**WESTBRIDGE UNIVERSITY LIBRARY** 1982·83 PL CC WW

This card must be produced each time a book is borrowed.

Loss of this card must be reported to the Library immediately.

Signature

**WESTBRIDGE UNIVERSITY LIBRARY** 1982·83 PL CC WW

This card must be produced each time a book is borrowed.

Loss of this card must be reported to the Library immediately.

Signature

**WESTBRIDGE UNIVERSITY LIBRARY** 1982·83 PL CC WW

This card must be produced each time a book is borrowed.

Loss of this card must be reported to the Library immediately.

Signature

**WESTBRIDGE UNIVERSITY LIBRARY** 1982·83 PL CC WW

This card must be produced each time a book is borrowed.

Loss of this card must be reported to the Library immediately.

Signature

*Small items pasted-up making more economical artwork*

*Note trim-marks showing where cuts are to be made*

slight tendency towards greying of the paper shows less on coloured stock than on white.

Artwork should where possible be done A4 size. Smaller items should be put onto A4 sheets, for example an A6 size postcard should be printed in fours. In order to save doing the same piece of artwork several times it is possible to do it once then reproduce it photographically and stick these together to form artwork.

Text for publications etc can be produced on an electric typewriter, a compositor or on a word processor. Headings can be added with dry transfer lettering. Logos can be reproduced in a number of ways. The original artwork could be photographically reproduced and pasted up to form an A4 sheet. This could then be printed and the results cut up and used on the artwork. Alternatively the photographed logo can be enlarged or reduced and the photographs themselves used on artwork. Another option is to have the logo produced by one of the dry transfer lettering companies. If this choice is made the library will need to provide the original artwork. Check with several such companies for competitive quotes. The resulting logos can then be applied in the same way as other lettering.

Although the market in this lettering is dominated by one major company there are a number of manufacturers in the field and it is worth comparing prices. Note too that it is possible to buy small sheets of some typefaces; useful for the odd job, particularly if it is a typeface to be used only once. The range of dry transfer letter is not restricted to letters. Most of the manufacturers produce a range of other sheets as well, such as rules, borders, decorative swashes etc. Also available are electrical and other symbols, and in the architectural field it is possible to buy sheets containing pictures of people, vehicles, trees etc. If this lettering is being used for the library guiding, remember that it is possible to buy sheets composed entirely of numbers. Some of the typefaces in this lettering are available in colours other than black, but the range of colours is small. If coloured lettering is needed the lettering machine is a better alternative. Other transfers include dot patterns and coloured film which can add tones to a floor plan for example. Although each sheet is quite expensive the effects that can be produced can be impressive.

Artwork or sections of artwork can be adjusted in size photographically. Artwork presented to the printer need not necessarily be the same size as the desired result. It may be much easier to do the artwork twice the size of the original particularly for small items such as a reader's card. The sequence in this case is

1  Produce the artwork twice the size of the final result.
2  Reduce the artwork photographically and produce several copies.
3  Paste up the copies on an A4 sheet.
4  Send to printers.

The printer can adjust larger sizes to A4 too. This may be useful if producing multiple copies of a large floor plan which is perhaps A2 size. Note however that it is the *proportions* which are important. They must be the same on the larger version as on the desired result.

# 11223345567 7

&

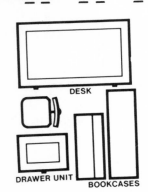

DESK

DRAWER UNIT BOOKCASES

$

?

ف ـفـفـف ق قـقـقـق ك ـكـكـكك

αβγδεζηθ
ΑΒΓΔΕΖΗΘ

DRY TRANSFERS
not just A to Z

абвгдежзий
АБВГДЕЖ

# DUPLICATING

In addition to printing and the photocopying, other processes are available. Stencil and spirit duplicators can be used to 'print' leaflets, handouts etc. The quality of these methods of reproduction is usually poor however, though they are cheap. One possibility is to use a stencil duplicator to add the text to a sheet which has a pre-printed heading on it, or to put duplicated sheets behind a printed cover. Poor quality printing does not encourage the potential reader to read it and tatty publications provide a negative image of the library. Stencil duplicating etc *can* be reasonable for short runs, but require a good typist to cut the stencil accurately and a skilled operator to get the best out of the machine.

# LETTERING FOR GUIDING

Other methods of lettering can be used for guiding as dry transfer lettering is expensive. Plastic lettering produced from coloured tape on a lettering machine is much more economical once the capital outlay on the machine has been met. Stencils too can be used and are very cheap. They do not need to look like the THIS WAY UP signs on packing cases. Look in the stationers for the more modern types of stencils which avoid the white lines between the parts of the letters. Yet another possibility is to use hand-lettered signs. This is the cheapest method of all, but does demand someone who can write well. Invest in proper lettering pens if this method is to be successful. Unfortunately the visual sophistication of most of the library's users means that hand-lettered signs are normally seen as crude and held in low esteem even when they are done well.

# SPECIALIST PRINTING

Printing on paper may not be the only printing required. If staff badges are to be produced in quantity it is necessary to contact a specialist badgemaker. If only a few are to be made get the wording printed and find someone who has a badgemaking machine locally, so that you can make them yourself. Carrier bags, T-shirts, balloons, car stickers *See Colour* are also possible promotional printing that the library may wish to *Microfiche* investigate. Printers and suppliers of these kinds of material can be found in the classified ads of magazines such as *Campaign*, a weekly publication aimed at the advertising industry. If your own library does not take it, get a recent copy on interlibrary loan. It does not matter which issue, as the small ads remain much the same from week to week. Ring round for quotes on this promotional material as the prices vary enormously.

Other specialist printing includes newspapers and broadsheets. It is worth getting a number of quotes for these, particularly from printers who specialise in this format. If there is a local newspaper it may be

WESTBRIDGE
UNIVERSITY
**LIBRARY**
STAFF

WESTBRIDGE
UNIVERSITY
**LIBRARY**
STAFF

WESTBRIDGE
UNIVERSITY
**LIBRARY**
STAFF

WESTBRIDGE
UNIVERSITY
**LIBRARY**
STAFF

WESTBRIDGE
UNIVERSITY
**LIBRARY**
STAFF

WESTBRIDGE
UNIVERSITY
**LIBRARY**
STAFF

WESTBRIDGE
UNIVERSITY
**LIBRARY**
STAFF

WESTBRIDGE
UNIVERSITY
**LIBRARY**
STAFF

Artwork for badges

possible for them to print a newspaper for the library at a competitive price simply because they can use their machinery at a time when it would otherwise be standing idle. In an academic library investigate the printers of the student paper if there is one.

## MATERIALS FOR GUIDING

Materials for guiding are more complex. The problems involved include durability, ease of fixing, safety from vandalism, ease of production. It is possible to buy commercially produced guiding systems but these are a) very expensive and b) not tailored to the specific needs of the library. Also they may not have the flexibility needed to guide something which is frequently moved round. It is amazing how often librarians move their stock! The basic materials for the home-made system include paper, card, wood and plastic/perspex. With these it is possible to assemble a sophisticated guiding system to meet the specific needs of each library; a system which not only looks good but is effective, flexible, and needs a minimum of skill to build. The various types of sign will be taken in turn and possibilities listed.

## EXTERIOR SIGNS AND GUIDING

Signs on the outside of buildings need to be durable. These can be made from plastic lettering glued to a plastic background. Alternatively preformed plastic letters can be fixed to the building itself. Where possible such signs should be out of reach to deter vandalism. Illumination can be by spotlights or could be inside large preformed letters. This latter method is often used in Northern Europe where the public libraries are not inhibited about advertising their whereabouts. Factors include cost both of production and fixing, which if high on a building can be expensive. The erection of any large sign on the outside of a building may need planning consent, particularly if it is to be illuminated. Check on this with the appropriate authorities and get permission *before* ordering the lettering.

*See Colour Microfiche*

## PLANS

Large plans and signs are best made of a sandwich of plywood, card or paper on which the information can be stuck, and a covering of clear perspex. The whole lot can be fastened to the wall using mirror screws. These are screws whose heads are covered with a domed chromium plated cap after they have been screwed in. They have the twofold advantage of looking better than conventional screwheads and providing a deterrent to vandalistic unscrewing. This sandwich approach gives flexibility in that the information can be easily changed as necessary without having to replace the entire sign each time.

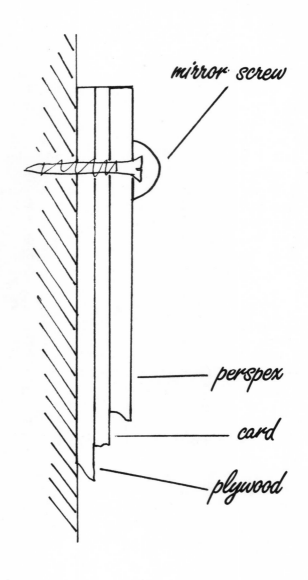

mirror screw

perspex

card

plywood

Sandwich construction for wall-mounted signs

Changes can be made simply by altering
the card layer

'Cake plans' can be simply made by painting the plywood backing sheet with the appropriate stripes of colour and adding adhesive letters, covering again with perspex sheet. Lettering for the guiding system should be of the stick-on variety, either bought as individual letters or produced on a lettering machine.

# SLAT SYSTEM

Other signposting is best done using a slat system. Examples of this can be seen on railway stations and in hospitals. It is a system that allows flexibility in the library in that when something is moved only the appropriate slats in the guiding need to be altered round and not the whole scheme. Additional slats can also be added as required. Commercially produced systems are expensive. Just as effective are white or coloured perspex strips with plastic lettering added. These can be suspended from the ceiling or stuck to walls.

# MOBILES

Other suspended signs include three dimensional mobiles. These can be made of card glued to thin wooden battens at the edges. Eighteen inch sides make a good size mobile. Mobiles have the advantage of being visible from a number of angles, not just by viewers immediately in front of them. Both these and the plastic suspended signs can be hung on nylon fishing line. Where the ceiling is made of acoustic tiles on a suspended framework the line can be fastened to the metal supports, but a neater solution is to make hooks from paper clips as in the diagram and to use these. This allows the signs to be moved or taken down for cleaning while still leaving the hooks in position. In conventional plaster ceilings hooks will have to be screwed in. Suspended signs should be hung well above head height.

*See Colour Microfiche*

# OTHER SIGNS

Signs to be fixed to internal walls can also be made of card laminated with plastic film. They can be fastened to the wall using double-sided tape or sticky pads and are usually durable enough. If they are to be fastened inside windows or glass doors there is no need even to add the plastic laminate.

Special letters for very large signs can be bought from commercial sign-makers. They will usually make up letters in any typeface so it would be possible to reproduce the library logo on a large scale if required. Alternatively the logo could be photographically blown up to the desired size. There is a limit to this process however, not only because of the size of photographic paper available, but also because the edges of the type begin to lose sharpness after a certain size. For a painted logo it would be possible to project the design onto a screen and draw round the outline.

| 2 Arts &Humanities | 1 Sciences | G Social sciences |
| --- | --- | --- |

*Cake Plans should be colour-coded for greatest effect.*

| | |
|---|---|
| ↙ **Exit** | |
| ↙ **Ausgang** | |
| ↙ **Sortie** | |
| ← **Platforms 1 to 12** | |

| | |
|---|---|
| **Out~patients** | → |
| **Maternity Unit** | ↗ |
| **All Wards** | ↗ |
| **Way Out** | ↘ |

*Slat Signs are familiar as guiding in many situations*

# MOBILE CONSTRUCTION

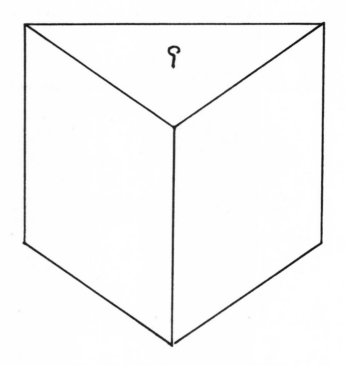

1 Glue squares of card to thin battens along top and bottom edges

2 Glue wood block to underside of top and screw in hook

3 Add top and bottom triangles

4 Strengthen edges with tape if necessary

5 Add lettering to sides

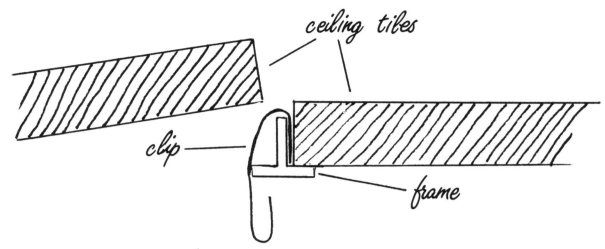

ceiling tiles

clip

frame

To hang items from a suspended tile ceiling

1   Partly straighten a paperclip

2   Gently push up the corner of a ceiling tile

3   Hook one end of the clip over the metal
    frame supporting the tiles

4   Lower the tile back into position

5   This leaves a neat hook to which to attach signs

6   If the nylon line supporting the sign is tied to
    a paperclip which is hooked to the one in the
    ceiling the sign can easily be removed for
    alteration or cleaning

Small freestanding signs on desks etc can often be made by slotting card into a perspex holder. A visit to a commercial signmaker's premises or to a firm making plastic lettering will suggest many possibilities. Look too at how other organisations cope with these problems. Restaurants and hotels are good sources of ideas for small perspex holders etc.

Door signs can be card laminated with plastic film, lettering on perspex or card under perspex covers. Tier guides can be made of card with lettering affixed. They are out of the way and do not usually suffer much damage. Like much of the guiding that is close to the bookstock they are likely to be changed at frequent intervals and therefore should not be made of expensive materials. They should be cheap enough so that if necessary they can be discarded if the movement of the bookstock renders them obsolete. Shelf guides if used should be made of card slotted into plastic holders which can be moved with the books. End guides should be pre-printed A4 sheets on which the relevant details can be typed. This allows the greatest flexibility where it is most needed. If the shelving system does not provide holders for end guides fasten them to the shelves with double-sided tape.

*See Colour Microfiche*

Coloured floor plans etc can be produced either by printing or photographically in black and white, with the colour added through the use of adhesive toned films. This is a rather fiddly job, but the results can be spectacular so it is labour that has a worthwhile reward. For details on how to apply the film see the manufacturer's catalogues. Practise first on some scrap paper!

The above techniques should enable the librarian to organise all aspects of the identity programme, even if he does not do it all himself. The production of the guiding described is not beyond the abilities of any technician or dextrous library assistant and the results can far transcend the simplicity of the materials and the techniques involved. As with most elements of the identity programme it is not the individual item that necessarily creates the greatest impression but the cumulative effect produced by the coordinated and systematic approach. This overall effect can hide any minor blemishes that may creep into some of the parts.

# Corridor

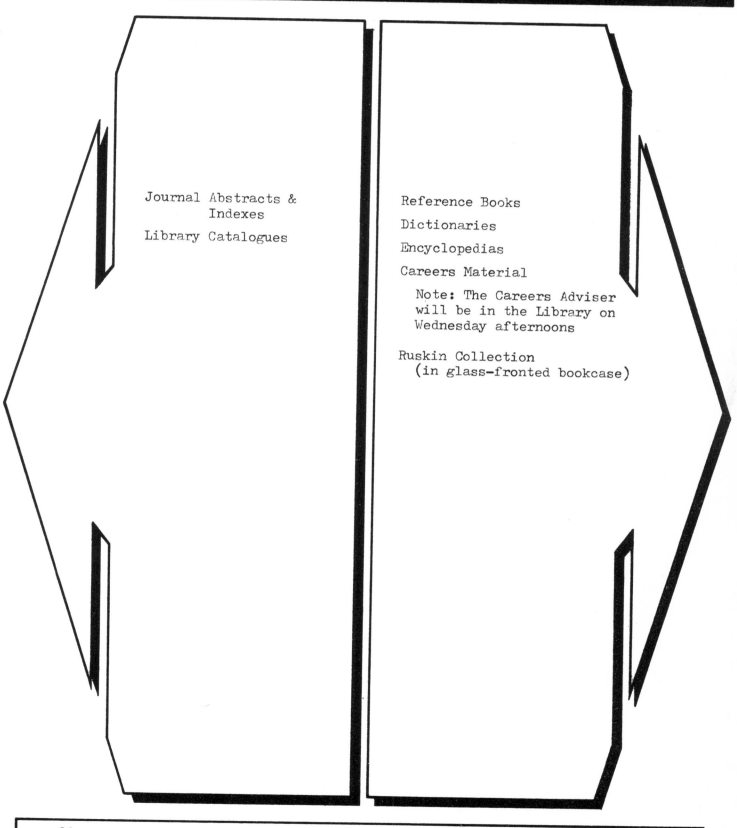

Journal Abstracts &
Indexes

Library Catalogues

Reference Books

Dictionaries

Encyclopedias

Careers Material

  Note: The Careers Adviser
  will be in the Library on
  Wednesday afternoons

Ruskin Collection
  (in glass-fronted bookcase)

**If you cannot find what you require, or need assistance, please ask a member of library staff for help.**

# 5.  Formats

The corporate identity programme will make use of material in a wide range of formats to get across its message. These should be decided on in advance and listed in the design manual. The following formats cover the range of the library's activities and a choice can be made from these. It is best not to use too many formats or this can lead to confusion of items and a dilution of the corporate identity approach. For example a range of ten A4 size publications will be more effective than 10 publications of assorted sizes. When choosing the sizes to use it is important to bear in mind the purpose of the item. The size of guiding for example will be determined by the need for legibility at a distance. The size of leaflets will be chosen with regard to several parameters, type size available, the audience, other publications in the range, economy of printing etc.

## EXAMPLES OF POSSIBLE FORMATS

1    *A4 sheet, printed on one or both sides.* This can be paper or card, and in a variety of colours. The shape and size of A4 paper however means that the print size must be fairly large in order to keep line lengths of an optimum size for good readability. Also plenty of space should be allowed in margins. Two columns of text are possible on A4 but the print size then becomes fairly small if lines that are *too short* are to be avoided.

   The main advantage of this size is that it is the most readily available paper size, and most printing processes will work economically with artwork of A4 size. In academic libraries it may be an advantage that the library's publications on this size paper will fit in students' clip-files, etc.

2    *A5 sheet, printed on both sides.* The A5 format, half the size of an A4 sheet, can produce a most pleasing appearance with a reasonably small type face. It it is to be printed on one side only two pieces of artwork can be placed side by side on an A4 sheet thus halving the costs of production. If both sides of the A5 sheet are to be printed the artwork for the two sides should be placed side by side. One printing plate only need then be made; the same plate is used to print both sides of

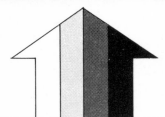

# Stadtbibliothek Wuppertal

# Hier ist die Wunschliste.

Aus dem Angebot der Stadtbibliothek interessieren mich:

(Gewünschtes bitte ankreuzen bzw. Einzelnes zusätzlich unterstreichen!)

### SCHÖNE LITERATUR

Abenteuer-, Agenten-, Spionage-, Geheimdienst-, Seeabenteuer-, Wildwestromane ☐

Frauen-, Familien-, Liebes-, Ehe- und Gesellschaftsromane ☐

Arztromane ☐

Berg-, Heimat-, Landschaftsromane ☐

Zukunftsromane ☐

Kriminalromane ☐

Religiöse Romane ☐

Heitere Romane, Humor, Satire ☐

Entwicklungsromane, Problematik des menschlichen Lebens ☐

Historische-, zeitgeschichtliche-, gesellschaftspolitische Romane ☐

Lebensbeschreibungen, Erinnerungen, Briefe ☐

Gedichte, Dramen ☐

Erzählungen ☐

Märchen, Sagen, Legenden, Fabeln ☐

Tierromane ☐

Experimentelle Literatur ☐

Mundart ☐

### SACHLITERATUR

☐ Nachschlagewerke, Schrift-, Druck- u. Buchwesen, Bildbände

☐ Erd-, Länder- u. Völkerkunde, Reisebeschreibungen

☐ Bücher über Wuppertal, Bergisches Land, NRW

☐ Geschichte, Zeitgeschichte, Kulturgeschichte, Volkskunde

☐ Recht

☐ Gesellschaft, Staat, Politik

☐ Wirtschaft

☐ Religion, Philosophie, Psychologie, Erziehung

☐ Literatur

☐ Bildende Kunst, Musik, Tanz, Theater, Film, Funk, Fernsehen

☐ Mathematik

☐ Medizin

☐ Naturkunde, Tier- und Pflanzenkunde, Astronomie, Geologie, Physik, Chemie

☐ Technik

☐ Photographie

☐ Landwirtschaft, Gartenbau, Hauswirtschaft, Kochbücher, Handarbeitsbücher

☐ Sport, Spiele, Basteln

### SONSTIGES

☐ Musikkassetten

☐ Sprachlernprogramme

☐ Spiele

☐ Zeitschriften

☐ Nur Großdruckbücher !

the A4 paper. When these are cut down the middle the A5 sheets will have been printed front and back. Again there are savings, in this case on artwork and plate production.

Advantages of the A5 sheet include its compatibility in a size of publications with an A4 sheet folded in half to make an A5 'booklet'. The A5 booklet is made from an A4 sheet so again the costs involved are low, and the production methods straight forward. If an A4 size single fold booklet is to be produced it would need an A3 size sheet. The printing of this may not be possible except by a sophisticated print unit able to handle such large paper sizes. Another advantage of A5 is that it is fairly small, easy to carry, and hence more likely to be picked up by the library users.

3    *A4 folded into smaller sizes*. The A5 simple fold leaflet has already been mentioned but an A4 sheet, with all its production advantages can be folded into a variety of other sizes to produce handouts of more convenient formats than the unfolded sheet. Two folds will produce a slim publication ideal for putting into a handbag or pocket. This gives six columns of text. Other items in the range could be one column wide or ⅔ A4 folded in half, since each of these will be the same size when folded. This produces a very flexible range but care should be taken when designing the artwork for the smaller items to make the most economical use of printing plates, artwork and paper.

4    *A4 and A5 booklets*. Single fold A4 booklets need to be printed on A3 size paper. A4 booklets are best made up of A4 sheets fastened together. A5 booklets can be made up of A4 sheets stapled through the middle. Booklets will look better if there is a separate cover, perhaps in a different colour paper or card. The fastenings can be staples or, more expensively, comb or clip bindings.

5    *Other small sizes*. The use of 5" x 3" stationery may be necessary in the library because of the availability of storage units to fit this size, but it is not the most economical size to produce. The best that can be done is to put as many pieces of artwork onto an A4 size, accepting that there will be some waste of paper or card.

A6 size can be used for postcards, four pieces of artwork to each A4 sheet. Bookmarks can be made four to an A4 sheet. The diagrams on pp 65-68 show possible layouts for printing one or both sides. Address labels can be A7 size, (on gummed paper).

6    *Larger sizes — A3 size*. This is probably the optimum size for a poster. Larger sizes get unwieldy and demand too much space for display. A2 size can be folded to form an A3 size newspaper. The production of these should be done by specialist printers with the equipment and expertise in this form of work. A3 size can also be folded twice to produce an A5 booklet which can be opened out to A3.

*See Colour Microfiche*

# WESTBRIDGE UNIVERSITY LIBRARY

# Reservations

If you want a book which is in our library catalogue, but not on the shelf, you may reserve it by filling in a yellow reservation card. These cards are obtainable from the information desks, and when completed, should be handed in there. If the book you require is not in the card or microfiche catalogue, you may request it through the Inter Library Loans Service (See Info. sheet No. 12)

On the card, fill in the author's name and initials, and the full title of the book, and edition if appropriate. At the bottom of the card, fill in your name and address or department, and your borrower number which is the 8 digit number on your library ticket. Fill in the deadline date, if relevant.

You will be sent a postcard when the book is available, and you should collect if from the Inter Library Loans and Reservations Section on the entrance floor. The book will be kept for you 10 days after the postcard is sent to you. The Reservation Staff will let you know if they cannot trace a copy of the book you require.

SHORT LOAN RESERVATIONS

If you want to reserve an item in the Short Loan Collection, do not fill in a reservation card. Check the Short Loan Catalogue, and quote the number written in red on the top right hand corner of the card to the library assistant at the Short Loan point. You will then be told if the item is on loan to another borrower, and whether any other readers have also reserved it. The assistant will reserve the item for you, and tell you when it is due back. The item will be kept for you for one hour after the time it is returned.

**M.J.M. 1.9.80**

# Stadtbibliothek Wuppertal

## Zentralbibliothek

mit Allgemeiner Informationsabteilung, Artothek, Mediothek, Musikabteilung
Kolpingstraße 8, Tel.: 563 23 73, Mo Di Do Fr 11-19 Uhr, Sa 10-13 Uhr

## Stadtteilbibliotheken mit Jugendabteilungen

Barmen ● Geschw.-Scholl-Platz, Tel.: 563 66 35, Mo Di Do Fr 11-13 und 15-19 Uhr, Sa 10-13 Uhr
Kinderbibliothek: Eingang Höhne, Tel.: 563 64 15, Mo Di Do Fr 11-18 Uhr
Beyenburg ● Am Kriegermal 23, Tel.: 619 05, Mo Do 10-13 und 14-18 Uhr
Cronenberg ● Hauptstraße 1, Tel.: 563 74 15, Mo Do 11-13 und 15-19 Uhr, Di Fr 10-13 und 15-17 Uhr
Langerfeld ● Odoakerstraße 2, Tel.: 60 56 99, Mo Do 11-13 und 15-19 Uhr, Di Fr 10-13 und 15-17 Uhr
Ronsdorf ● Markt, Tel.: 563 72 25, Mo Do 11-13 und 15-19 Uhr, Di Fr 10-13 und 15-17 Uhr
Uellendahl ● Röttgen 155, Tel.: 70 84 43, Mo Do 11-13 und 15-19 Uhr, Di Fr 10-13 und 15-17 Uhr
Vohwinkel ● Rubensstraße 4, Tel.: 563 73 44, Mo Do 11-13 und 15-19 Uhr, Di Fr 10-13 und 15-17 Uhr

## Jugendbibliotheken

Barmen ● Rödigerstraße 126, Tel.: 563 61 46, Di Do 11-13 und 14-17 Uhr
Cronenberg ● Jung-Stilling-Weg (Schulzentrum Süd), Tel.: 563 52 45, Mo Do Fr 8-14 Uhr, Di 8-17 Uhr, Mi 8-12 Uhr
Elberfeld ● Marienstraße 7 (Jugendheim), Tel.: 563 23 48, Mo Di Fr 11-13 und 14-17 Uhr
Reichsgrafenstraße 34/38 (Schule), Tel.: 563 26 06, Mo Fr 11-13 und 14-17 Uhr
Robert-Daum-Platz, Tel.: 30 78 21, Mo Di Do Fr 11-18 Uhr
Heckinghausen ● Meyerstraße 34/36 (Schule), Do 11-13 und 14-17 Uhr
Langerfeld ● Hildburgstraße 250 (Schule), Tel.: 563 69 92, Do 11-13 und 14-17 Uhr
Oberbarmen ● Liegnitzer Straße 62/64 (Schule), Tel.: 563 61 83, Mo 11-13 und 14-17 Uhr
Ronsdorf ● An der Blutfinke 70 (Gesamtschule Ronsdorf), Tel.: 563 52 22, Mo 8-15 Uhr, Di 8-13 Uhr, Mi Fr 8-13.30 Uhr, Do 8-17 Uhr
Uellendahl ● Am Dönberg 46 (Schule), Tel.: 77 99 32, Di 11-13 und 14-17 Uhr

The rooms in the Library at Psalter Lane are named after people connected with the School of Art. We are often asked about them, and the brief biographical notes overleaf may be of interest.

## Young Mitchell 1811-1865

Was Headmaster of the School from 1846 to 1863. It was under his direction that the School first began to flourish, and he had considerable influence on a group of artists and designers who were known as 'The Sheffield School'. This group included Godfrey Sykes, James Gamble, William Ellis, and a number of other Sheffield students who later went on to work in London with Alfred Stevens.

## Godfrey Sykes 1825-1866

Was a pupil and later a teacher at the Sheffield School of Art. He was much influenced by Mitchell and by Alfred Stevens. He is best remembered for his decoration of the South Kensington Museum. There is a memorial to him in Weston Park, near the Mappin Art Gallery.

## Alfred Stevens 1817-1875

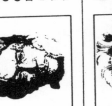

Came to Sheffield in 1850 to work for Hoole & Co. on the recommendation of his friend Young Mitchell. While in the city he influenced many students in the School, many of whom later worked with him in London. His most famous work is probably the Wellington Monument.

## Omar Ramsden 1873-1939

Was a student at the School of Art. He established himself as a silversmith in London at the turn of the century with A C E Carr, also a former student of the School.

## Frederick Varley 1881-1969

Was a student at the School of Art. He emigrated to Canada in 1912 and there met the artists with whom he formed the Group of Seven, including Arthur Lismer, who had also been a student at Sheffield.

Written by John Kirby, Site Librarian, Psalter Lane Site

Edward Bond

# Gerettet

Edward Bond:

Gerettet. In: Spectaculum. 11. 1968.

Gerettet. In: Kindlers Literaturlexikon. Erg. Bd.
Werke A.-Z. Sp. 971-973.

Das englische Drama der Gegenwart. Interpretationen.
Englische Literatur der Gegenwart in Einzeldarstellungen.
Peter Iden: Edward Bond.
Franz Norbert Mennemeier: Das moderne Drama des Auslandes.
S. 183-192.
Ernst Wendt: Moderne Dramaturgie.
U. Mehlin: Die Behandlung von Liebe u. Aggression in Edward
Bonds ,,Gerettet".
In: Jahrbuch d. Dt. Shakespeare-Ges. (West). 1970. S. 132-159.
Warten auf waswofür? Edward Bonds Stück ,,Gerettet" an den
Münchner Kammerspielen. Von Ernst Wendt.
In: Theater heute. Jg. 1967. H. 6, S. 8-12.

Über Aggression:

Du tust mir weh.
Aggressionen im Leben der Kinder und Jugendlichen.
David Mark Mantell: Familie und Aggression.
Hans-Peter Nolting: Lernfall Aggression.
Peter Scheiner: Wie du mir ...
Aggressionen und Konflikte im Alltag.
Andrea Weingarten: Umgang mit aggressiven Verhaltensweisen.

Horst Laube

# Der Dauerklavierspieler

Horst Laube: Der Dauerklavierspieler. 1974.

Gerd Jaeger: Warum ist das so, wie es in diesen Stücken ist?
In: Theater heute. 15. 1974. 11. S. 34-37
Heiner Mueller: Der Dramatiker und die Geschichte seiner Zeit.
(Ein Gespräch). In: Theater heute. 16. 1975. Sonderh. S. 114-123.
Günther Rühle: Ein Zustand, in den man hineingerät.
In: Theater heute. 19. 10. S. 48-49.
Lukas Rüsch u. Hans Dieter Jendreyko: Wir Kleinbürger.
In: Theater heute. 19. 10. S. 46-47.

## Schwarz auf Weiß

Begleiter zum Spielplan der Bühnen.

Was man Schwarz auf Weiß besitzt,
kann man getrost nach Hause tragen. Zum Beispiel
Bücher und Zeitschriften aus der
Stadtbibliothek mit ihren 20 Zweigstellen.
Für vier Wochen und kostenlos. Aber man kann
genauso auch Noten, Schallplatten
und Tonbandkassetten entleihen. Eine
ausgezeichnete Möglichkeit für den Opern- und
Theaterfreund, sich auf ein Bühnenereignis
vorzubereiten. Musik noch einmal zu hören.
Nachzulesen. Nachzudenken.

Die Zentralbibliothek mit ihrer großen
Musikabteilung finden Sie in der
Kolpingstraße 8, Wuppertal-Elberfeld.
Telefonische Auskunft
unter der Rufnummer 563 23 73.

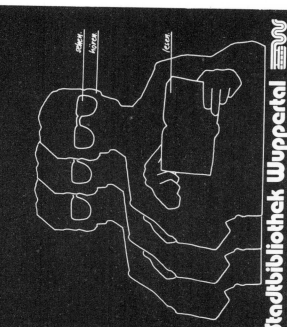

Stadtbibliothek Wuppertal

Ernst Toller

# Hoppla, wir leben

Ernst Toller:

Gesammelte Werke in 5 Bänden. 1978.
Prosa, Briefe, Dramen, Gedichte. 1961.

Modernes deutsches Drama. Kritiken und Charakteristiken.
Bd. 1-2.
Kindlers Literaturlexikon Bd. 3, Sp. 2140-2142.
Carel Ter Haar: Ernst Toller. Appell oder Resignation?
Sigrid Vietta und Hans-Georg Kemper: Expressionismus.
Hannah Arendt: Über die Revolution.
John Dunn: Moderne Revolutionen.
Der Fall Toller. Kommentar und Materialien.
Manfred Durzak: Das expressionistische Drama.
Ernst Barlach. Ernst Toller. Fritz von Unruh. S. 81-151.
Karl Griewank: Der neuzeitliche Revolutionsbegriff.
Kurt Lenk: Theorien der Revolution.
Paul Noack: Die manipulierte Revolution:
von der Bastille bis in unsere Zeit.
Guenter Rohrmoser: Revolution – unser Schicksal?
Georg Siebers: Psychologie der Revolution.
Gerhart Binder: Das Kaiserreich und die Weimarer Republik.
Wolfgang Elben: Die Weimarer Republik.
Helmut Heiber: Die Republik von Weimar.
Hans Herzfeld: die Weimarer Republik.
Helmut Hirsch: Experiment in Demokratie.
Zur Geschichte der Weimarer Republik.
Sigmund Neumann: Die Parteien der Weimarer Republik.
Günter Pössinger: die Zwanziger Jahre.
Chronologie eines turbulenten Jahrzehnts.

Johann Wolfgang von Goethe

# Clavigo

Johann Wolfgang von Goethe:

Werke. Bd. 1-14. 1948-64.
Werke. Bd. 1-6. 1965.
Werke. Bd. 1-6. 1977.
Clavigo. 1917.

Clavigo. In: Kindlers Literaturlexikon. Bd. 1. 1969. Sp. 2675-2677.
Pierre Augustin Caron de Beaumarchais:
Die wahre Geschichte des Clavigo. Memoiren.
Peter Boerner: Johann Wolfgang von Goethe in Selbstzeugnissen
und Bilddokumenten.

# PUBLIC ADMINISTRATION

## Some useful class numbers

| | |
|---|---|
| Administration theory | 350 |
| Central government | 351 |
| Constitutional law | 342 |
| Educational admin. | 371.2 |
| Foreign governments: administration | 354 |
| Great Britain: administration | 352.042 |
| International relations | 327 |
| Local government | 352 |
| Philosophy | 100 |
| Political history | 320.9 |
| Political philosophy | 320.1 |
| Political science | 320 |
| Political theory | 320.01 |
| Practical politics | 329 |
| Public administration | 350 |
| Social administration | 360 |
| State and citizen | 323 |
| State systems | 321 |
| US Federal and State Government | 353 |
| Economic history | 330.9 |
| Economics | 330 |
| Ethics | 172 |
| Management | 658 |
| Operational research | 001.424 |
| Sociology | 301 |
| Town planning | 711.4 |
| Transportation planning | 711.7 |

WESTBRIDGE UNIVERSITY LIBRARY POND STREET SITE

October 1980

# PUBLIC ADMINISTRATION

## Some useful class numbers

| | |
|---|---|
| Administration theory | 350 |
| Central government | 351 |
| Constitutional law | 342 |
| Educational admin. | 371.2 |
| Foreign governments: administration | 354 |
| Great Britain: administration | 352.042 |
| International relations | 327 |
| Local government | 352 |
| Philosophy | 100 |
| Political history | 320.9 |
| Political philosophy | 320.1 |
| Political science | 320 |
| Political theory | 320.01 |
| Practical politics | 329 |
| Public administration | 350 |
| Social administration | 360 |
| State and citizen | 323 |
| State systems | 321 |
| US Federal and State Government | 353 |
| Economic history | 330.9 |
| Economics | 330 |
| Ethics | 172 |
| Management | 658 |
| Operational research | 001.424 |
| Sociology | 301 |
| Town planning | 711.4 |
| Transportation planning | 711.7 |

WESTBRIDGE UNIVERSITY LIBRARY POND STREET SITE

October 1980

**WESTBRIDGE UNIVERSITY**
**LIBRARY**
PSALTER LANE SITE
Psalter Lane

Telephone
56101
Ext. 30

We have been unable to trace a copy
of this item so far. Please see no.

1. Do you still require this item?

2. Do you wish us to apply to another library?

3. Do you wish us to apply abroad? This will
   entail some delay.

4. Please supply a photocopy of your source
   of reference.

**WESTBRIDGE UNIVERSITY**
**LIBRARY**
PSALTER LANE SITE
Psalter Lane

Telephone
56101
Ext. 30

We have been unable to trace a copy
of this item so far. Please see no.

1. Do you still require this item?

2. Do you wish us to apply to another library?

3. Do you wish us to apply abroad? This will
   entail some delay.

4. Please supply a photocopy of your source
   of reference.

**WESTBRIDGE UNIVERSITY**
**LIBRARY**
PSALTER LANE SITE
Psalter Lane

Telephone
56101
Ext. 30

We have been unable to trace a copy
of this item so far. Please see no.

1. Do you still require this item?

2. Do you wish us to apply to another library?

3. Do you wish us to apply abroad? This will
   entail some delay.

4. Please supply a photocopy of your source
   of reference.

**WESTBRIDGE UNIVERSITY**
**LIBRARY**
PSALTER LANE SITE
Psalter Lane

Telephone
56101
Ext. 30

We have been unable to trace a copy
of this item so far. Please see no.

1. Do you still require this item?

2. Do you wish us to apply to another library?

3. Do you wish us to apply abroad? This will
   entail some delay.

4. Please supply a photocopy of your source
   of reference.

"Get those Library books back before the end of term, or I'll have to send the boys round. . . ."

Library books may be returned to any Site Library

WESTBRIDGE
UNIVERSITY
LIBRARY

7   *Folders.* In academic libraries it is common to provide some form of folder in which the publications can be collected. This allows students to pick up those in which they are interested, or librarians to make up packs of information leaflets to suit particular courses. Obviously such folders must be slightly larger than the leaflets. They can be printed on one side of card sheets and then folded and stapled to make up the folders. Alternatively standard wallet files can be overprinted with the library logo, etc. The use of folders and separate leaflets allows far more flexibility than a booklet describing all the library's services. Certain information leaflets will not need changing for a number of years, others will need rewriting each year. The use of leaflets allows only those which need rewriting to be redesigned. The folders can be produced on a higher quality card with economies gained from a long print run. The leaflets inside could be produced more cheaply, but the overall package would still look good.

8   *Unusual formats.* Balloons, carrier bags, badges, T-shirts and other promotional printing can be done by specialist printers and manufacturers. If the library provides the artwork the costs will be reduced.

9   *Publications for sale.* The formats here will be similar to those listed in earlier sections, but additionally these may be microfiche, microfilm, photographs, cards etc. Microfiche and microfilm formats need to be produced by commercial companies specialising in this form of work. If there is to be an accompanying text with the microfilm some type of packaging needs to be designed to put the two together. Fiche can be slotted into a wallet inside a booklet.

10  *Guiding formats.* There are more possibilities in the sizes of guiding than for publications since in most areas items will need to be individually made. Some elements of the guiding programme can benefit from being made in standard paper sizes so that they can be reproduced in quantity. However, such items as end guides, floor plans etc which are to be repeated frequently should be in a standard size. Colour can be added to printed outline floor plans with coloured film. If only a limited number are needed they could be reproduced photographically and again the colour added in film.

Signs of the same type should all be the same size. A decision should be made on the sizes and typefaces to be used for each type of sign, eg destination signs, guide signs etc. If coloured card is being used note there will be limits on the length of signs because of the standard card sizes. Plastic signs can be made any size but slat signs 30" x 4" will probably be adequate.

Destination signs can be the same size, or could be larger to show their importance.

11  *Microfilm, tape slide productions and other multimedia*

*See Colour Microfiche*

*See Colour Microfiche*

*See Colour Microfiche*

| Flap | Back | Front |
|------|------|-------|

4cm

31cm

22cm

Layout and dimensions of a folder to hold A5 size leaflets

Fold in flap and fasten with a staple

*packs need to be in boxes or specially designed folders.* Postcards are best produced in A6 size so that they can be printed from A4 stock; greetings cards can be made A6 or A5 size. As with other publications and stationery the use of standard paper sizes should not be forgotten in producing publications for sale. A slightly larger margin on a reproduction map to bring it up to A4 size does not mar the finished product, but costs less than one ½" smaller because there has been no need to put the sheets through the guillotine. The main points in deciding on the formats the library will use are:

1   How do the various publications, stationery etc relate to each other in size?
2   Do all the items conform to the standard paper sizes, and if not can they be produced with minimum wastage by sticking multiple copies of artwork together onto A4 sheets?
3   What materials are available and do these have any effect on how the resulting items will look? For example flat signs made of card need protection if they are to remain clean and unwarped.
4   What production methods are available? There is no sense demanding an A3 broadsheet if the printer cannot cope with this size.

Whatever formats are chosen however it is ultimately not the size which creates the identity for the library. It is the coordination of each item with the same sizes being used, identifiable ranges of publications similar in appearance, and uniformity in guiding.

# 6. Layout and Design

The arrangement of material on the printed page and the design of all aspects of the identity programme should be given a great deal of thought. In order to achieve consistency of approach it is useful to draw up a series of grids for layout in the various formats that the library intends to use for its publications etc. These grids will ensure that the position of type area, logo, headings etc will be uniform and of acceptable proportions. The advantage of the grid system is that it is not necessary to rethink the layout each time something is produced since the framework for the design will already be available.

The actual size and proportions of the grids are largely a matter of taste and can be adjusted to meet local needs. Factors to take into account include:

1   Type size. Try to avoid lines which are either too long or too short. Both affect legibility.
2   Size of margins. Do not skimp on margins and do not attempt to use every millimetre of space on the page. Narrow margins look mean and the page will appear too densely packed with print. This is offputting to the reader.
3   Positioning of any fixed items. For example leave a space in the top-left corner for the logo, put page numbers in the middle of the bottom margin.
4   Grids for the guiding system should allow variant positions of arrows. ·
5   If signs etc are to be fastened to walls, ensure that the screw-holes will not obscure any of the message.
6   Leave space round headings so that they stand out from the text.
7   In general allow plenty of space. It can be tempting to cram as much as possible onto the page or sign, but this can be self-defeating. The empty area around the message is nearly as important as the text itself in communicating effectively.

     Do not crowd the information together but allow the reader to assimilate the message before going on to the next piece of information.
8   Look critically at the layout of everything with which you come into contact; books, signs, advertisements, packaging. Decide if the general impression of each item is pleasing,

and if so try to analyse what the elements are that make it 'good design'. If it is an unattractive item, look for what it is that detracts from a pleasing effect. Try to consider how you would have dealt with that particular design problem. This is not always an easy process, but is valuable for the librarian to attempt to develop a feel for design so that he can then make use of these skills in his work in the library.

The following pages show a variety of grids and layouts for a range of potential library items.

## A4

Text area

A4

A5

Text area

A4

# 7. Typography

There is often a feeling of mystique attached to the selection of typefaces. The jargon used by typographers is ancient and often incomprehensible to the layman, or even to the librarian with only a limited knowledge of this highly specialised subject area. It is not the intention here to go into great detail on this topic which is the subject of many books, but the librarian should know some of the criteria which should influence his choice of typefaces, and some of the technical terms used.

In most cases the following headings are sufficient in order to make an effective choice:

1 Availability
2 Serif or sans-serif
3 x-height in relation to point size
4 Openness

All of these factors have a bearing on legibility, on the overall appearance of the printed material, and the general character of the identity programme. Perhaps more than any other single factor the choice of typeface will affect the viewer's feelings about the programme.

1 Availability. It is essential that the typeface or typefaces chosen for the identity programme are readily available in a range of media. Rub-down transfer lettering, plastic lettering, stencils etc. There is no point in deciding to use an obscure typeface for guiding the library if each letter has to be hand-drawn on each notice. For this reason a typeface like Helvetica or Univers is ideal since it is easily obtained.
2 Serif or Sans-serif. The choice here is largely one of taste. There are arguments both ways over which form of typeface is the most legible. In terms of the identity programme these criteria are probably irrelevant. When reproducing lettering however it is probably worth remembering that a sans-serif face is easier to draw, easier too to use with transfer lettering as there are fewer little bits to knock off, and easier for sign manufacturers to produce in card or plastic.
3 x-height. The x-height is as its name suggests the height of letters such as a, o, x, e. The point size is the overall height of the letters. Look for a typeface with a reasonably large x-height. This will be

more legible than one with a small x-height in relation to the point size. The larger x-height face will appear larger.

4    Openness. This refers to the amount of white space in letters such as a, o, e, p, etc. and is related to the x-height to some extent. Look for a typeface where there is a reasonable amount of openness. Again it improves legibility.

The choice of typeface for guiding will probably be different from that chosen for use in publications, logo etc. In choosing a typeface for guiding the librarian should remember that the signs will be in a range of sizes, using a variety of materials. The signs may all be made in the library or may be a mixture of home-made and ready-made. Look at examples of guiding in use in railway stations, hospitals, airports etc. The typeface used is usually Helvetica or a variant of Helvetica. This is a sans-serif face, easy to reproduce, available in a wide range of sizes in transfer lettering, available as plastic stick-on lettering, available on lettering machines, easy to cut out of materials such as hard plastic or card. The x-height and openness make it a legible typeface. Moreover it has the added advantage of being a typeface associated in many people's minds with guiding, signposting etc because of its common use for this purpose. Where signs are available for sale they are usually available in Helvetica or something similar. Given that it has been chosen by so many other organisations which have put a lot of effort into research in this area it would seem sensible for the library to adopt this typeface for its guiding too.

The choice of typefaces for publications and texts will depend on factors such as available typesetting or electric typewriter golfballs. Within reason the choice for text is an aesthetic one from those available to the library from those sources. Consistency is probably the best criterion. The use of the same typeface for all the library's publications, whatever that typeface is, will act as a coordinating factor and create a uniformity consistent with the identity programme. Headings in the text, titles for publications etc, may be produced on the artwork from transfer lettering, in which case there is an enormous choice. Choose sensibly. Avoid obvious mistakes such as fairground type lettering, or letters made of rustic logs, or High Victorian advertising graphics. If the text is a serifed face, choose a serifed face for the headings. Try to find a typeface that will match the text to some extent in weight. The headings should obviously stand out, but they should not overpower the text. But again it is the consistent use of one typeface for headings and titles that will create the effect overall and the librarian should not agonise too much over the selection. Make some mock-ups of publications and see if they look right. Try them out on a group of critics if in doubt. The logo or standardised form of the library's name is where the typeface freak can really go wild. Unlike the typefaces for other purposes it is not easy to change if a wrong choice is made. It is essential therefore to choose a typeface which looks good in the particular wording of the library name. Several typefaces should be tried, using both all upper case and a mixture of upper and lower case, using different size typefaces for different

point size

x height

openness

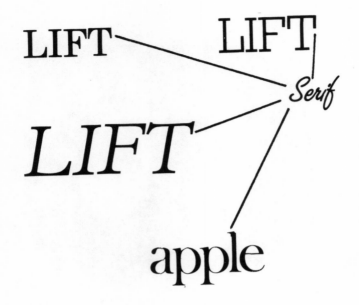

LIFT  LIFT

LIFT

*Serif*

apple

**LIFT**        **Lift**

**apple**

*Sans-Serif*

# Library ↑

A typeface such as Helvetica Medium is a good choice for guiding

elements of the name, even different typefaces. Although the criterion of availability should be borne in mind, the logo will be reproduced as a unit, not as individual letters. The logo should be distinctive, otherwise it has no point, and it should be pleasing to look at, though of course that is a subjective view. If in doubt err on the side of plainness and simplicity. There is less likely to be a mistake with a logo that is straightforward and plain. Such a logo is also less likely to appear dated. Remember that the logo will be in use for some time, will permeate all the elements of the identity programme and that it will be on show to a lot of people a lot of the time. Logo design is highly complex. It is therefore worth employing a designer to do this if no other element of the programme. Before it is put into general use the logo should tried out on a variety of uses to test reaction to it. Be particularly aware of the problems that can arise with a non-verbal form of logo. Although this may get round the problems of typeface it may itself have an obscure meaning, or may mean different things to different people.

For the librarian attempting to choose a safe set of typefaces for his identity programme it is probably worth keeping to typefaces in use in other organisations which appear pleasing, which are legible and available. Many large institutions will have put a lot of effort into their choice. The library can benefit from their research and play safe at the same time as knowing that the library's choice will at the very least be an adequate one.

# 8. Guiding the Library

## GUIDING OUTSIDE THE LIBRARY

Guiding the library starts outside the building in the surrounding streets. There are standard signs for directing pedestrians to the public library which are the responsibility of the local authority. Approaches should be made to them to ensure that this guiding is adequate. In a college or university such guiding will usually be provided by the administration of the institution and will be in a form compatible with other guiding on the campus. The library building itself should be identified by a sign visible from a reasonable distance. The sign for the library should include the library logo if possible and should be illuminated at night. Where the library is inside another building and is not a separate unit it is essential that some guiding is provided from the entrance of the building to the library itself. There should also be some indication at the entrance that the library is in the building, with details of opening hours. Once the user has been guided to the door of the library he should find another notice telling him he has got there. Again the opening hours should be given in case he missed the sign at the main entrance.

*See Colour Microfiche*

Where the library is in its own building there should be clear indications of where the entrance is. This will often be obvious from the way that paths lead and from the architectural features of the building but it is nevertheless worth checking that this is so and providing an additional sign if necessary. Be particularly careful about this if there is a carpark at the back of the library where the users will be seeing the building from an angle different from the view from the street.

## AT THE ENTRANCE

At the entrance there should be a notice giving the name of the library and the opening hours. The notice for the opening hours should include space to slot in details of holiday closing and in the case of an academic library details should be given of variant hours in term and vacation. Other notices appropriate at this point include details of access if this is restricted, warnings about security systems if applicable and alternative means of access if necessary for disabled persons in wheelchairs. The door to the library should leave no doubt as to

*See Colour Microfiche*

The Library is
on floor 8

LIBRARY

*Signpost the library*

whether it should be pulled or pushed. Pulling a door that should be pushed and vice versa does seem to infuriate many people and a small sign on each side of the door can save a lot of irritation. Ideally the door should have at least one glass panel so that people can see others trying to use the door at the same time. This is necessary to avoid injury as people open the door. If the door is predominantly or totally glass however it is necessary to mark the door in such a way that it is clear that the door is there. This can be done by fixing notices to the glass, but a better solution is to fasten a strip of coloured tape across the panel of the door at eye level. This is particularly necessary in public libraries where old people are frequent users. Children are very vulnerable to accidents with glass doors and it is essential that the doors are marked at their eye level too. If the entrance is formed of a number of doors it may be useful to designate some for entrance and others for exit. If this is done the doors must be marked clearly on both sides. The verbal messages can be reinforced by the use of the standard road symbols for No Entry and One Way. These pictograms are readily available as stick-on signs. If doors are not in use they must be marked as such and not just left locked. It appears to be a hazard of twentieth century life that one is continually trying to enter doors which either should be pulled instead of pushed or that are locked instead of open. Trying to open a locked door causes irritation to the user and if more than one in a row of doors is locked the library can soon have a large number of needlessly angry readers. There is no sense in antagonising the users before they even get into the library.

## THE ENTRANCE AREA

Once the users *are* inside the library it is essential to provide them with some guidance. Unless the entrance area is designed to provide an exhibition space or room for waiting it is a good idea to move the readers away from the doors as soon as possible. The basic destinations of most library users can be predicted and only these should be guided at this stage. Some of these destinations might be:

1    Book returns. This is the first thing most people do on entering particularly in a public library. It should be clearly visible and there should be a sign indicating it.

2    Information point and visitor reception. Many people will be entering the library to make an enquiry. They should be directed somewhere where they can do this. It may be a separate reference library or just an enquiry desk. Many people will be entering the library for the first time to enrol. It is necessary to indicate where they should go for this. People wishing to enrol should not be passed from one desk to another. This does not give a very good impression of the efficiency of the library. It is better to guide them to their destination from the entrance. Others will be entering the library as visitors. These may be other librarians, students,

# push

## STAFF ONLY

## DOOR NOT IN USE

## Exit

*Door signs*

| | |
|---|---|
| **REFERENCE LIBRARY** | ↑ |
| **ADULT LENDING** | → |
| **CHILDREN'S LIBRARY** | ↘ |
| **COFFEE BAR** | ↘ |
| **TOILETS** | ↗ |

*Guiding near the entrance*

councillors, etc wishing to see someone on the library staff, or coming to attend a meeting. It is worthwhile directing such visitors to a specific point from which they can be redirected or met by the librarian responsible. Staff at this enquiry desk should be aware each day of expected visitors and who to contact when they arrive. This simple device creates an air of efficiency far outweighing the small amount of effort required to implement it. Where large numbers of people are expected to attend a meeting in the library some form of sign should be provided for the occasion to direct them to the appropriate room. eg 'Philately Society Meeting in Lecture Room 2 on Floor 3', 'Marxist Society Seminar in the Classroom on the Lower Floor'. Boards with movable letters are useful for this.

3    The other destinations of people entering the library will be the main departments, bookstacks, reading rooms etc. The guiding at the entrance area should be as broad as possible. It is not necessary to give too many details unless there are stairs or lifts in the immediate vicinity. If there are only a few possible routes that users can take at this stage then guide them with generalised terms such as Lending Library, Reference Library, Children's Library, etc, or even All Departments. Guiding here should be easily seen and easily read. If the detail or size of sign demands that the users stop walking to scrutinise it then it needs redesigning. The aim is to move people towards their destinations, not have them clog up the entrance to the building while they try to decipher where to go.

## SECOND STAGE GUIDING

The next stage in the guiding process is to provide choices. These will come at junctions, stairs, lifts. If the building is on more than one level the users should be provided with spatial guiding such as a 'cake' plan or slat guiding to show what level they need to move to. If the library is on one floor some form of plan could be provided. Both cake plans and floor plans can be colour coded and the colours used should follow through to the destination. For example if one part of the plan is coloured blue the guiding relating to that part of the library should be blue also, as a visual reinforcement of the message.

## LEVELS

Where several levels are involved it is essential to tell the user what floor he needs before trying to orientate him on the particular floor. Floor plans should not be provided except on the floor to which they relate. Cake plans should be provided inside lifts to amplify the rather bald statements of floor numbers usually provided by the manufacturers. Note the various ways of numbering floors, and the problems

| | |
|---|---|
| This Floor | 800 - 999 |
| 4 | 700 - 799 |
| 3 | 500 - 699 |
| 2 | 001 - 499 |
| 1 | Exit |

Simple Cake Plan

001 – 499 ↑

500 – 999 ←

JOURNALS ↗

that can arise in those buildings with basement or underground storeys and in buildings where the entrance is not on the ground floor. Consider too the possibilities where buildings are linked together at different levels.

Ensure that the guiding overcomes any spatial confusion. There should be a clear indication of which floor has been reached outside each lift, visible when the lift doors open to further confirm to the user that he has reached the correct level. Similar signs should also be placed on landings and at the entrance to stairs. If the exit from the building is not at ground level signs should be provided at the same points indicating this, eg EXIT ON FLOOR 2.

## FLOOR GUIDING

Having got the user to the right level it is now necessary to get him to the correct part of the floor. Floor plans can be used to do this but if the library is not too large it may be as effective to provide hanging signs or mobiles which can be seen from the entrance to the floor. Alternatively directional slat signing can be provided. This should give more detail than the guiding at the entrance.

The destinations themselves should be marked so that the user clearly knows he has got to where he was going. Do not lead users into dead ends or guide them halfway to their destination and then stop providing signs. Where the lines of travel are obvious as in a corridor it is only necessary to provide guiding at decision points such as junctions. Where the situation is more fluid as in a large open-plan library signs may need to be repeated more often and for the user to feel most secure it should always be possible to see the next sign so that he is never in doubt. Where the library is divided into a number of rooms it is useful to provide a plan and key to what is in each. This can be colour coded by room both on the plan and in the guiding. If the library is at all complex the floor plan should be repeated at frequent intervals, at the entrance to each room for example, or at each block of shelving, with a YOU ARE HERE pointer. These plans need only be A4 size, reduced from the main floor plan. This will help the user orientate himself in the library.

There have been a number of suggestions about floor plans. Ideally they are best viewed flat, oriented in the correct directions, so that straight ahead on the plan is straight ahead on the floor itself. This may not always be possible however. The best way to solve the floor plan problem is to look for some feature in the library which can be made distinctive on the plan. This might be a staircase, or windows or blocks of shelving. The shape of the floor might be enough. Some authorities have suggested that floor plans should be redrawn depending on the way that the user is facing. This can lead to considerable confusion and although the logic behind this idea is sound, in practice it does not work. As an analogy consider the map of the world with which everyone is familiar; turn this map upside down and then try to find where the various countries are. It is not easy, yet there is no reason

*See Colour Microfiche*

*See Colour Microfiche*

84

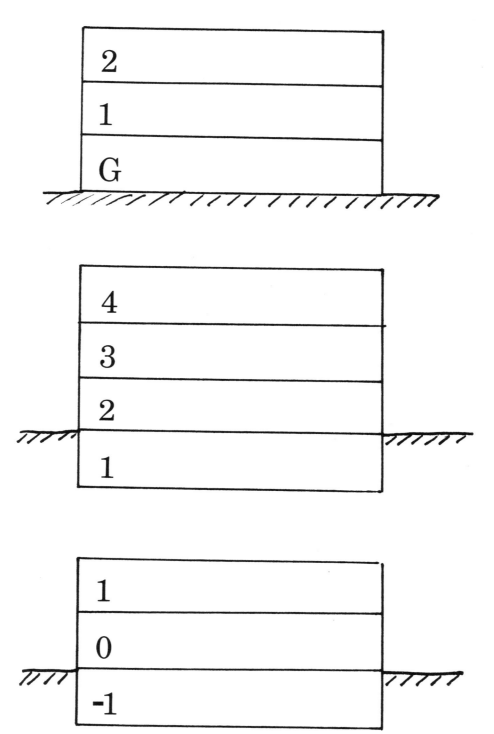

Floor numbering

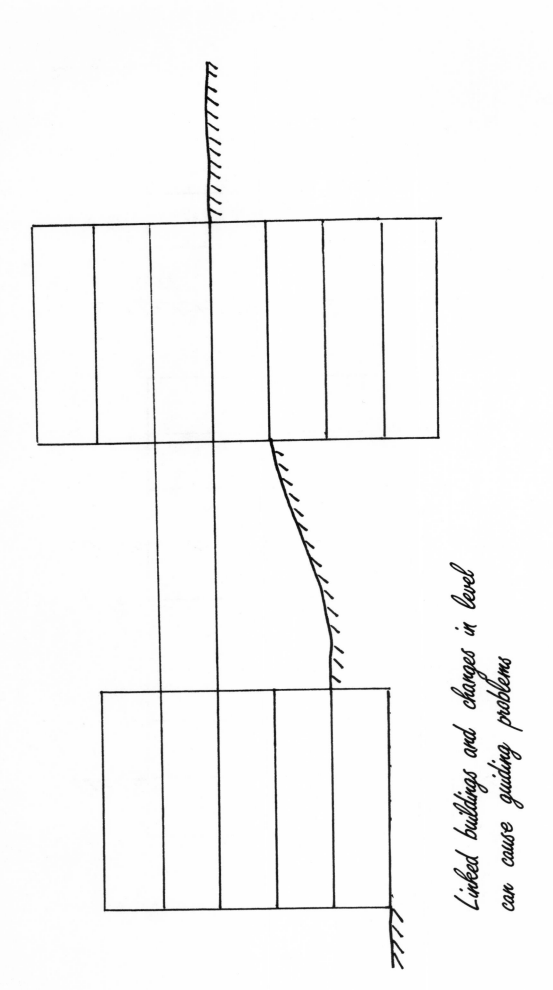

Linked buildings and changes in level
can cause guiding problems

# WESTBRIDGE UNIVERSITY LIBRARY
## PSALTER LANE SITE
## Floor plan

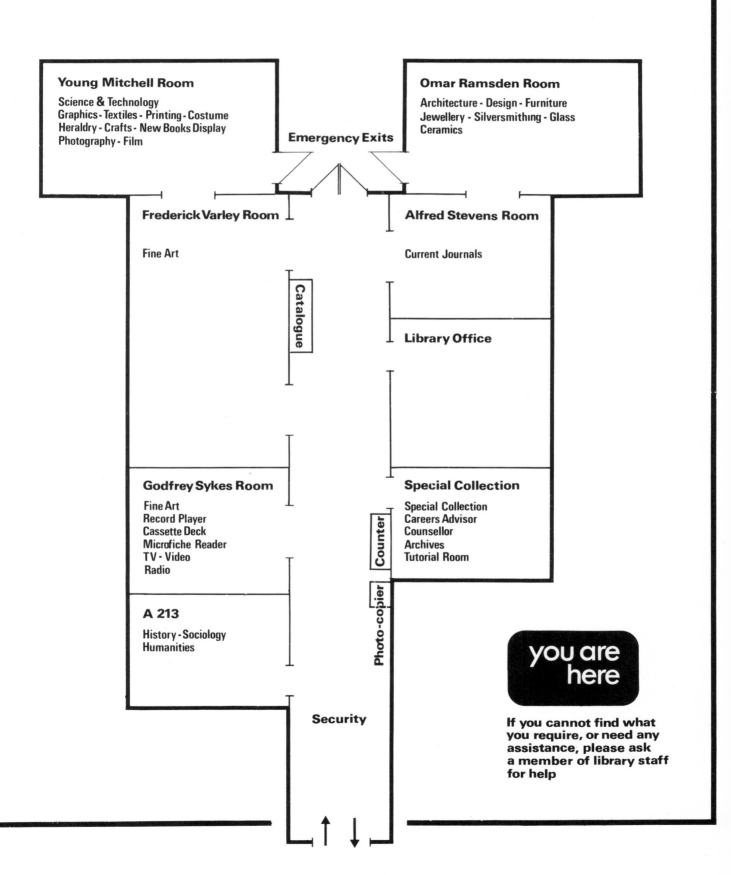

**Young Mitchell Room**

Science & Technology
Graphics - Textiles - Printing - Costume
Heraldry - Crafts - New Books Display
Photography - Film

**Emergency Exits**

**Omar Ramsden Room**

Architecture - Design - Furniture
Jewellery - Silversmithing - Glass
Ceramics

**Frederick Varley Room**

Fine Art

**Alfred Stevens Room**

Current Journals

Catalogue

**Library Office**

**Godfrey Sykes Room**

Fine Art
Record Player
Cassette Deck
Microfiche Reader
TV - Video
Radio

**Special Collection**

Special Collection
Careers Advisor
Counsellor
Archives
Tutorial Room

Counter

**A 213**

History - Sociology
Humanities

Photo-copier

**you are here**

**Security**

If you cannot find what
you require, or need any
assistance, please ask
a member of library staff
for help

# Wegweiser durch die Zentralbibliothek

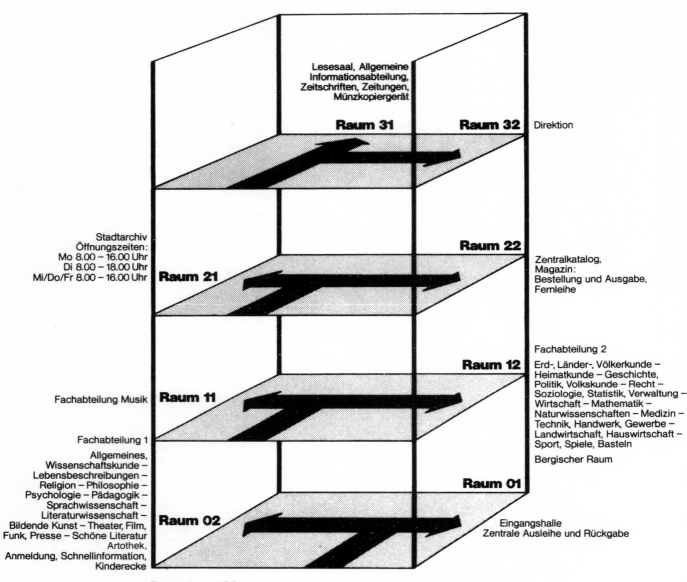

Lesesaal, Allgemeine
Informationsabteilung,
Zeitschriften, Zeitungen,
Münzkopiergerät

**Raum 31**          **Raum 32**     Direktion

Stadtarchiv
Öffnungszeiten:
Mo 8.00 – 16.00 Uhr
Di 8.00 – 18.00 Uhr
Mi/Do/Fr 8.00 – 16.00 Uhr          **Raum 21**

**Raum 22**

Zentralkatalog,
Magazin:
Bestellung und Ausgabe,
Fernleihe

Fachabteilung 2
Erd-, Länder-, Völkerkunde –
Heimatkunde – Geschichte,
Politik, Volkskunde – Recht –
Soziologie, Statistik, Verwaltung –
Wirtschaft – Mathematik –
Naturwissenschaften – Medizin –
Technik, Handwerk, Gewerbe –
Landwirtschaft, Hauswirtschaft –
Sport, Spiele, Basteln

Fachabteilung Musik          **Raum 11**

**Raum 12**

Fachabteilung 1

Bergischer Raum

Allgemeines,
Wissenschaftskunde –
Lebensbeschreibungen –
Religion – Philosophie –
Psychologie – Pädagogik –
Sprachwissenschaft –
Literaturwissenschaft –
Bildende Kunst – Theater, Film,
Funk, Presse – Schöne Literatur
Artothek,
Anmeldung, Schnellinformation,
Kinderecke

**Raum 02**

**Raum 01**

Eingangshalle
Zentrale Ausleihe und Rückgabe

Treppenhaus 1. OG:
Wuppertal aktuell, Öffentlicher Fernsprecher

Raum 13: Studio
Wuppertaler Tagespresse,
Funk- und Fernsehinformationen

Treppenhaus 2. OG: Ausstellung

Treppenhaus 3. OG: Forum

Aufzug in alle Stockwerke,
Zugang im EG durch Raum 02
Kinderwagen und Rollstühle: Nebeneingang

why this map of the world is less accurate or less valid than the conventional one with North at the top. Drawing the floor plans for the library the same way up each time allows the user to become familiar with the shape of the library and to form a mental picture of it, just as he does with the world map. He can then orientate himself on the actual floor, keeping in his mind the image of the plan by using the distinctive features in front of him. From the librarian's point of view, not only are such plans more effective, they are also cheaper to produce as they can be printed in large numbers from one master. The printed plan should also include the wording "You are here", but without the arrow, which can be added pointing to the appropriate place when the plans are fastened to the walls.

The simplest of these plans is a line drawing. This can be greatly improved if colour coding can be added, and the result will generally be found to be very effective. There are other ways of drawing plans however using special techniques which give an impression of three dimensions. These can look very good, but they require a skilled draughtsman to produce and for many people they can be confusing because they are unfamiliar.

Having guided the user to his destination, do not forget that he may now wish to go somewhere else in the building, or to the exit. The way out should be clearly marked, with signs visible from all parts of the floor if possible. The directions for the user going to other destinations can be catered for by providing some or all of the following:

1  Mobiles or hanging signs for other destinations on the floor.   *See Colour Microfiche*
2  Floor plans to direct him to other areas on the floor.
3  A cake plan to direct him to services on other floors.
4  Signs to lifts, stairs to get him to other floors.

Combinations of these should enable the user to get to any part of the library from any other part.


# DOORS

All doors in the library should be marked to show their purpose, even if they are kept locked. This allays the curiosity engendered by a closed door! Cupboards or stores can be marked Cleaner's Store or similar. Nameplates on doors should be consistent with the rest of the guiding and the forms of names should be decided on and used consistently, eg Gill Kaye or Ms G Kaye. Doors which the users are expected to enter should have a glass panel in them so that they can see the place into which they are going. Most people are hesitant about opening a closed door to enter an office area, so if users are expected to go into an office to make enquiries it is best if the door can either be kept open or have a clear notice asking the user to enter.

# EMERGENCY SIGNING

Details of fire/emergency exits should be clearly signposted and the guiding etc should be worked out with the appropriate fire or safety officers. Such guiding should be in a standard format, usually green lettering on a white background and the other guiding in the library should *not* be in these colours. Notices giving details of what to do in an emergency should be posted at intervals in prominent positions. One should be by each lift and staircase and one should be at the counter, enquiry desk etc., wherever staff are usually stationed. Separate notices for the staff on what to do in an emergency should also be posted in prominent positions in staff areas, including the staffroom.

The key to getting people about the building is to provide systematic guiding:

1   Do not force people to stand reading detailed instructions. Use a large type size and use broad terms. Save the detail until it is necessary.
2   Get the user to the correct level in the library before giving floor plan details.
3   Provide guiding at all junctions and other decision points.
4   Keep to a limited range of types of guiding so that the user becomes familiar with the pattern of the system. Be consistent with lettering, size of signs, colours etc to further reinforce the pattern.
5   Provide guiding in lifts and on stairs.
6   Provide signs to indicate when destinations have been reached.
7   Repeat floor and cake plans at frequent intervals.
8   Guide the user to the exit and other destinations within the library.
9   Ensure that emergency guiding is adequate.

The above points should enable the user to find his way round the library as a building. The next chapter will consider the way to guide him in the library as a resource for information.

# 9. Guiding the Collection

In this chapter the emphasis is on guiding the library or a series of collections, and on helping the user to exploit the stock.

For a person trying to make effective use of the library there are a number of sources of assistance. The first of these is the layout of the library itself. If the library is arranged in some logical way then it is easier to find things. For example a library on several floors might start its classification scheme on floor 1 and progress up the top floor eg. Floor 1 001–399, Floor 2 400–699, Floor 3 700–899, Floor 4 900–999. Alternatively the library might take verbal subject divisions, relegating the classification scheme to second place – eg. Floor 1 Social Sciences, Floor 2 Pure Sciences, Floor 3 Applied Sciences, Floor 4 Arts and Humanities. This would probably mean that the classification scheme would not run in sequence, in which case some key to what numbers were where is necessary. Or the library might be divided by function – eg. Ground Floor, Lending, First Floor, Reference, etc. A logical arrangement is invaluable to the user, provided that the logic is clear!

The second major resource is the library staff. Information points should be provided at key areas in the library so that users can make enquiries. Such information points should be manned as much as possible, or if not manned this should be indicated, with details of where to go to get help. Other possibilities at the unmanned information point include a display of information to which the user can refer, and could include floor plans, details of services on posters, leaflets, etc, and details of where to get help. Such information points seem most useful when the reader is browsing and does not have an urgent, specific problem or query. In these latter cases the reader seems to prefer being able to go up to a librarian and get an instant answer. Some means of staff identification is useful. This can take a number of forms. In academic libraries it can be particularly useful to identify key staff, subject librarians for example, by photographs. This identification gives the user an advance idea of whom he may wish to speak to on a *See Colour* particular problem. It also says something about the library as a *Microfiche* whole, showing that the library staff wish to be seen as specialists, and that they care about the services provided for the users. There can be considerable staff resistance to photographs however. It is essential that the pictures are professionally taken and should be of a resonable size. The usual passport-size offerings seen in many libraries are duly nicknamed "mugshots", and do little either for the morale of the staff or in the interests of identifying them to the users. Underneath the good photograph should be the name and job title or some description of the work the librarian does. Do not use job titles if these will not mean much to the ordinary library user. Use terms which he will understand, such as "Subject Librarian – Art and Design", "Journals Librarian" etc. Job titles such as "Bibliographic Services Coordinator" either need rewriting in understandable language or amplifying with a description of what the librarian does. It is not usually necessary to put in details of jobs, responsibilities etc with which the library user will not come into contact. The key people and jobs to identify are the ones which affect the public's use of the library.

The second means of identifying staff is to provide nameplates at information points etc. This tells the user who he is actually talking to, provided that the nameplate is changed when staff go off duty!

Library staff should also wear some form of identification such as a badge to show that they are library staff. This should apply to all, including the most junior assistants. In many libraries it is often difficult to know who is a member of staff and who is not unless they happen to be sitting at a desk. Since many enquiries may be directed at staff when they are away from a named desk they should be identifiable. Unfortunately most library users want to ask questions in parts of the library where there are no information points – for example amongst the shelves, at the catalogue, wherever they encounter a specific problem. Also many users seem reluctant to approach a librarian at an enquiry desk. They may feel that their question shows an exceptional ignorance, or may be too trivial with which to disturb the busy librarian poring over his papers and bibliographies. Such people will far rather ask a library assistant. Observation has shown that the people most likely to be asked questions in the library are assistants at an issue desk, because they are obviously library staff; assistants shelving, because they are obviously staff and happen to be where the user has the problem, at the point where he is looking for a book; staff at the catalogue, again because it is a place where many users have problems. Usually these queries are relatively straight forward – "Where are the 699s?" "What does this mean in the catalogue?" "What do I do if the book I want is out?" All library staff should be trained to answer such basic questions, and to be able to identify the sorts of questions they need to pass on for more expert help at the information point, and they should themselves be identifiable by wearing a badge. This measure, coupled with effective guiding of the building and services (see Chapters 8 and 10) should reduce the trivial enquiries made to professional librarians and thus make more effective use of their time and abilities. As with photographs however there is often resistance to badges. Some staff seem almost ashamed to admit to the public that they actually work in the library. This feeling is not reserved to junior staff either. Staff should be identifiable as such so that users can ask them questions, whether they are timetabled to be at an information point or not. Isn't it one of the librarian's main functions to help the library users? The manager at the local

See Colour
Microfiche

92

supermarket does not fail to tell his customers where goods are if they ask him, so why do some librarians think it is beneath them to answer readers' enquiries?

Other claims made against the wearing of badges include the danger of facetious remarks, principally to young female staff, the reluctance to be known by name to all and sundry and the fact that they damage clothes.

All these fallacious reasons for not wearing badges can be contested. It is probably most economical *not* to provide individual named badges, but something general which mostly identifies the person as Library staff. If damage to the clothing can be proved there are alternative forms of badge (though more expensive) which use a clip rather than a pin.

The prudent librarian will keep a large supply of badges in his desk available for when his staff manage to leave theirs at home!

The next major resource in using the library is the catalogue. The library catalogue is one fo the most expensive single elements in the infrastructure of the library, given its costs in production and upkeep. For its costs it is also probably the *least used* element. For many readers it is baffling, for even more it is something to be avoided if at all possible. Yet as all librarians know it is the key to the collection. The librarian's task therefore is to make the catalogue comprehensible to all the library's users. There are two areas here which need attention. Firstly the layout and form of the catalogue itself, and secondly the notices, and hand-outs which explain the catalogue to the user.

The physical format of the catalogue will have been decided alredy, sheaf, card, fiche or on-line via a terminal etc. Every effort should be made to make the catalogue as understandable as possible by highlighting important elements such as class marks and location dates. Most users are put off by the use of codes to indicate in which library a book is held. This is a particularly relevant practice in public libraries using a fiche catalogue, with branch location data being given by simple letters. The spelling out of branch names may cost more but there seems little point in putting the data in at all if it is not understandable except to library staff. The layout of the entries should be made with care, using indentation and spacing to create the most legible form. Data of use to Library staff only, such as control numbers should be buried in the entry and not highlighted to provide confusion for the ordinary users. The layout of card catalogue entries too, though following standard practice, may also benefit from revision.

Even if it is not possible to alter the layout of the catalogue entries it is essential to provide clear guidance on the meaning of the catalogue data. There are various possibilities here, including leaflets which can be given out to users, but whether these are provided or not, there is still a need for some form of guiding at the catalogue itself. This should be clear and written without undue librarianship jargon. The notice should explain at least the following:

1   The difference between the various parts of the catalogue,

# Catalogue

**For help in using this catalogue please ask**

If you cannot find what you require, or need assistance, please ask a member of library staff for help.

# card catalogue

This Catalogue is being superceded by the computerised library catalogue, which can be accessed via the terminals on each floor of the library.

This Catalogue does NOT give details of any items added to the library since April 1978, and many older books are also in the new catalogue.

It is therefore ESSENTIAL to look in BOTH catalogues during this transition phase.

including details of any cut-off points for new and old catalogues – eg "Books added to stock after 1978 will be found in the Microfiche Catalogue".

2 How to operate the machine if it is on fiche, film or other mechanical format.

3 How to use the various catalogues to find an item.

4 What part of the catalogue entry is important to find the item on the shelves, eg "The book is shelved at the number in the top right corner of the catalogue card." "Orange catalogue cards indicate that the books are shelved at the Management Library at Totley. Grey catalogue cards indicate that the books are shelved at the Art and Design Library at Psalter Lane."

5 The general layout of the stock in the library, with an indication of what class numbers are where. In a multistorey library this could be a cake plan. In a multisite academic library where there is a subject specialisation some detail of this should be given.

6 Finally there should be some details of where to get help – eg "If you need any help in using the catalogue please ask for assistance at the Information Point."

*See Colour Microfiche*

The other aspect of guiding the collection is the signposting of the bookstock itself. Details should be provided of any special collections eg Local Studies, Parliamentary Publications, Statistical Data Collection, European Documentation Centre, Children's Library, Company Reports, British Standards etc. Some of this information may be in the form of leaflets, but details on a notice should also be provided to alert users to their existence.

Details of the layout of the main areas of bookstock should be given on sign posts, eg Lending Library, Reference Library, Children's Library, Music Library etc, with details of class numbers if these do not run in sequence or if they are split up through being in different parts of the library.

The guiding to the bookstock should be at several levels.

*See Colour Microfiche*

1 Broad guiding to get the user to the correct level or area of the floor.

2 More detailed guiding nearer the destination.

3 Tier guides. These should be above each bay of shelving and should be visible from a reasonable distance. These headings should be fairly general. The aim is to give an indication of which bays of shelving the user will be interested in. In blocks of shelving where tier guiding would not be visible larger signs should indicate the subjects and class numbers in the block.

*See Colour Microfiche*

4 End guides. These should be A4 sheets indicating in detail what is on the shelves on either side. The easiest method is to print blank sheets and type on the detail. In the event of books being moved round substantially the old sheets can be discarded and a new one typed.

# WESTBRIDGE UNIVERSITY LIBRARY

THE STOCK OF THE UNIVERSITY LIBRARY IS SPLIT
BETWEEN THE 5 SITE LIBRARIES ROUGHLY ACCORDING
TO SUBJECT, REFLECTING THE TEACHING ON EACH
SITE.

| | | |
|---|---|---|
| COLLEGIATE CRESCENT | : | EDUCATION, HEALTH STUDIES |
| POND STREET | : | SCIENCE & ENGINEERING, SOCIAL SCIENCE & BUSINESS |
| PSALTER LANE | : | ART & DESIGN |
| TOTLEY | : | HUMANITIES |
| WENTWORTH WOODHOUSE | : | GEOGRAPHY & ENVIRONMENTAL STUDIES, P.E. & HUMAN MOVEMENT |

FOR FURTHER DETAILS ABOUT THE STOCK OF THE SITE LIBRARIES,
OR ABOUT OTHER LIBRARIES IN WESTBRIDGE, PLEASE ASK AT ANY
INFORMATION DESK.

# DO YOU WANT TO KNOW MORE ABOUT THE EUROPEAN COMMUNITIES?

There is a European Documentation Centre serving the Sheffield region at Sheffield City Polytechnic Library, Pond St., Sheffield.

It is a collection of most of the official publications and working documents of the European Communities

This is a reference collection available for use by members of the public

WENTWORTH
UNIVERSITY
LIBRARY
SPRING STREET SITE
SPRING STREET
WENTBRIDGE

Leaflets are available from:   Grahame Wills, Sheffield 20911 ext 494

Architecture

Gardening    635

*Tier guides*

# Class № Guide

630.1 — 635.942

635.942 — 636

For further information please ask at the information desk or consult the subject index in the reference area

5    Shelf guides. The value of these is doubtful. By the time the reader has got to the correct set of shelves he is probably going to find the book he wants without too much difficulty. Shelf guides may be useful if they are kept up to date with the movement of stock, otherwise they are more of a hindrance.

6    Other aids – A simple but effective aid to assist in finding items such as journals which are stored elsewhere than might have been expected is to provide a dummy book with a message on it. This gets round the problem of readers not using the catalogue but going straight to the shelves and then not finding the whole run eg: Dummy book shelved next to bound volumes of a journal – "Art in America. Volumes 1913–1969 on microfilm only."

Notices should be placed between rows of shelves indicating which way the class numbers run, and between blocks of shelving so that users can follow the sequence of the classification scheme.

Notices such as end guides should carry a message like "If you cannot find the book you are looking for please ask the library staff for help" in order to reinforce the idea in the user's mind that the staff are there to help him.

*See Colour Microfiche*

Where colour coding has been used on floor plans the guiding should follow these colours. Where no colour coding has been used the guiding should be in one colour only.

*See Colour Microfiche*

Bookmarks. These can be subject based, giving details of useful class marks or could advertise specific collections or services.

Other leaflets and handouts can be produced on the same basis. These should coordinate with the rest of the design policy. Such publications may include current awareness services, new books lists, bibliographies, booklists etc.

Audio visual presentations, user education etc. These fall outside the scope of this book, but obviously they play a significant part in explaining the library's collection to its users, particularly in an academic library. The corporate identity programme however should be a continuous visual replacement of what is taught in the user education programme.

# CHEMISTRY

## Some useful class numbers

| | |
|---|---|
| Analysis | |
|   General | 543 |
|   Organic | 547.3 |
|   Qualitative | 544 |
|   Quantitative | 545 |
| Chemistry | 540 |
| Chromatography | 544.92 |
| Inorganic chemistry | 546 |
| Kinetics | 541.39 |
| Laboratories | 542 |
| Molecular structure | 541.22 |
| Organic chemistry | 547 |
| Organic synthesis | 547.2 |
| Organometallic chemistry | 547.05 |
| Photochemistry | 541.35 |
| Physical chemistry | 541.3 |
| Physical organic | 547.1 |
| Quantum chemistry | 541.28 |
| Spectroscopic analysis | 544.6 and 545.83 |
| Stereochemistry | 541.223 |
| Valence; bonding | 541.224 |

**October 1980**

## Other class numbers which may interest you

| | |
|---|---|
| Chemical physics | 539 |
| Chemical technology | 660 |
| Crystallography | 540 |
| Explosives; fuels | 662 |
| Industrial chemistry | 661 |
| Industrial organic chemistry | 668 |
| Mineralogy | 549 |
| Spectroscopy | 535.84 |

## See also bookmarks on

Biology
Metallurgy
Physics

Viele Kinder lernen die Bibliotheken in ganz jungen Jahren kennen, wenn ihre Eltern mit ihnen dort Bilderbücher, Märchen oder Geschichten zum Vorlesen holen. Gehen sie zur Schule, bekommen sie auch einen eigenen Ausweis. Bibliothekare helfen ihnen bei der Auswahl von Büchern, und sie lernen, in den Regalen selbst zu entdecken, was sie gerne lesen oder hören möchten. Das hilft ihnen sehr, wenn sie heranwachsen und für die Schule oder für ihre Berufsausbildung Literatur immer nötiger brauchen. Mühelos finden sie den Weg zum Bibliotheksangebot für die Erwachsenen, zu den über eine halbe Million Büchern und anderen Materialien aller Gebiete, die jedem Bürger dieser Stadt zur Verfügung stehen. In 20 Bibliotheken. Für lebenslanges Lernen, für praktisches Tun oder zum Entspannen in freien Stunden. Kostenlos auch für die Erwachsenen.

Ist Ihr Kind dabei? Und Sie selbst?

Stadtbibliothek Wuppertal

A5 sheet folded to make an A6 leaflet

# WESTBRIDGE
# UNIVERSITY
# LIBRARY

## European Documentation Centre

1983

Pond Street Site

# 10.  Services and Procedures

The third area of guiding the library concerns services and procedures. It is important to explain the services available to the user, partly so that he may make use of them, partly to remove some of the basic queries made to library staff. Explaining how to borrow a book to fifty different readers individually can be trying, and is a waste of library resources. There is a limit too to the amount of information that users may take in at one go, particularly when they join the library, and are being bombarded with a lot of new information, new environment, etc, and some reinforcement of the message is necessary. Since some users seem incapable of remembering even how many books they may borrow it is not surprising that they do not know by heart the details of the full range of the library's services!

When the design programme is being drawn up a list of services and procedures should be prepared and guiding and, where appropriate, leaflets or handouts should be produced. The following list of services is a starting point, but each library system will add others:

    Enrolment/Reservations/Requests. (Decide on terminology and stick to. Ditto for Journals/Periodicals/Serials.)
    Interlibrary Loans
    Photocopiers
    Microfilm/Microfiche readers
    Audiovisual equipment
    Computer terminals
    Storage areas such as Rolling Stacks, map cabinets etc
    Book Return point
    Book Issue point
    How to borrow a book
    Library rules and regulations
    Details of other libraries in the area:
    No smoking, no eating, drinking etc.
    Fires/Fire extinguishers/First Aid.
    Toilets, Coffee bar, Exhibition area, car parking facilities for the handicapped, sale of publications, display of information about the library and its services, information points/desks, Book box for return of books when library is closed. Student Counsellor . . . The County Council's Consumer Protection . . . etc.

# WESTBRIDGE UNIVERSITY

**WESTBRIDGE UNIVERSITY LIBRARY**
COLLEGIATE
CRESCENT SITE
Collegiate Crescent

Telephone
665274
Ext. 216, 217

**WESTBRIDGE UNIVERSITY LIBRARY**
POND STREET SITE
Pond Street

Telephone
20911
Ext. 487, 486

**WESTBRIDGE UNIVERSITY LIBRARY**
PSALTER LANE SITE
Psalter Lane

Telephone
56101
Ext. 30

**WESTBRIDGE UNIVERSITY LIBRARY**
TOTLEY SITE
Totley Hall Lane

Telephone
368116/369941
Ext. 273

**WESTBRIDGE UNIVERSITY LIBRARY**
WENTWORTH
WOODHOUSE SITE
Wentworth

Telephone
742161
Ext. 220, 240

# WESTBRIDGE UNIVERSITY LIBRARY

## GUIDE TO THE FIVE SITE LIBRARIES

# 5

MEMBERS MAY USE THE FULL FACILITIES AT ANY SITE LIBRARY

All of these should have some form of guiding associated with them. In the case of equipment this should include instructions for use and details of whom to go to for help in the event of any problems. The Library rules ought to be displayed in full somewhere in case someone asks to see them.

But there is not normally any need to do more than put them up in a reasonably public place. On the whole it is probably best not to draw a great deal of attention to them as they are usually written in an off-putting legalistic way.

Specific rules however may be highlighted and be the subject of their own posters – "Do not eat, drink or smoke in the Library" for example. In general No Smoking signs should be in the standard pictogram. There are also standard pictograms available to show the location of fire extinguishers, first aid boxes etc. It is useful to have a list of first aiders, fire marshalls etc available at each information point, issue counter etc. Pictograms can also be used for public telephones, toilets and for facilities for disabled and handicapped persons. Details of other libraries in the area should include information such as "The Polytechnic Library is available for reference use by members of the general public on application to the Librarian".

Posters can be a useful way of highlighting particular services, or asking readers to do things, eg Bring your books back before the end of term.

Posters can also be designed to advertise the library's own publications, or for an exhibition, meeting or concert etc in the library. For these latter events it is worth having a basic design which can then be overprinted with specific information.

One of the most confusing and complex parts of the readers' use of the library is enrolment and the first borrowing of books. The following points are worth consideration:

1    It is necessary to guide people to the correct part of the library for enrolment. In the case of an academic library it may be possible to enrol students when they register for courses. In the public library make it clear where readers enrol. This will be their first experience in the library – do not leave them floundering about wondering where to go.

2    The formalities of filling in an enrolment card, the checking of identity etc and the issue of some form of library ticket will depend on the issue system in use. The design of form and tickets should coordinate with the identity programme.

3    The information given to the user. It is essential to give the new user some piece of paper with basic details such as: the number of books that can be borrowed, library opening hours, address and phone number and general information about the library and its services. This can then be referred to at leisure. It is helpful if these details are also displayed on a notice in the library. The user should also be told any particular details that may be relevant to him – eg "We don't charge fines to pensioners". Staff should then point out to the

*See Colour Microfiche*

*See Colour Microfiche*

# WESTBRIDGE
## UNIVERSITY
# LIBRARY
## PSALTER LANE SITE

Out of consideration for other readers wishing to work, please do not make undue noise in this room.

Designed to fit in a perspex stand on a table

new user the general layout of the library eg "The Lending Library is on this floor" referring them to the various plans. If there is time it is a nice touch to ask if the reader is looking for anything specific or for books on particular subjects. He can then be given directions for finding at least something that he wants, and can then find his way round at leisure. It is *not* very helpful just to give the user his ticket and abandon him with no further information. It is also rude and shows an uncaring attitude on the part of the library. Unfortunately it is not uncommon.

One particular service which could benefit from attention to its "guiding" is the mobile library service. The schedules of the service should be attractively produced and made available in village post offices, or notice boards etc. In addition small plasticised notices could be fixed at each stop. These innovations would add considerably to this already useful service providing continuous reminders of the library even when the vehicle itself is not there.

The aim in guiding services and procedures should be to make the library self-sufficient so that users do not have to ask questions about these basic elements. The form of the guiding should follow that used in guiding the library building and guiding the collection, and in reality the three elements will be fused into one guiding system.

# Mobile Library Service

The Mobile Library stops here once each fortnight.

For details of dates and times please telephone

Barchester 8439 ext 257

## Barsetshire Libraries

# Mobile Library Service

Route 6

Monday, Week B


Harpole
   New Road, outside no 4         9.30
    Nag's Head                  9.45
    Council houses            10.20
Box Cottage                  11.00
Ullathorne Lodge          11.20
Ullathorne House          11.35
Whitegates Farm           12.10
      "       "   Cotts       12.25


Plumstead
   School                  1.30
   Briar Close             2.10
   Drake's Rd             2.35
   Royal Oak             3.05
   Post Office            3.30
   Churchview            4.05
Barrett's Farm           4.40

# Barsetshire Libraries

| PHYSIOLOGY ↑ | PATHOLOGY ← | PHOTOCOPIER ↓ | EXIT ↓ |
|---|---|---|---|

# 11.  Library Stationery

Library stationery is frequently the Cinderella of the library's design. Publications and guiding will often be considered but stationery is usually far less well done. Yet stationery is a very important element in the identity programme. It is a part of the library that reaches out far and beyond the immediate vicinity of the building. Letter headings, compliment slips, address labels, for example, can give an impression of the library and its services far from the library itself. More homely stationery for internal staff use only should also get the full design treatment. Library staff will benefit from the corporate identity, economies may be achieved by changes in design, and there should be a general rationale that no area of the library's activity is exempt from or does not deserve the attention of the identity programme.

*See Colour Microfiche*

Changes in library stationery however may not be attained in the same time scale as other parts of the programme. It is wasteful to destroy old stationery, if it can still be used, and the most sensible way forward is to redesign each item as it comes near to the end of existing stocks and needs replacement. Alternatively the designs can be prepared and the artwork held ready until reprinting of the stationery becomes necessary when the new design can be introduced. A list of all the library's forms should be compiled and examples collected when the corporate identity programme is being developed. In a library with branches or many sites special attention should be paid to the use of different stationery for the same purpose. Often it will be found that different parts of the library are using completely different stationery to say the same thing. This duplication should be eliminated in the interests of economy. Where possible the same stationery wording should be used with different library addresses as appropriate. Consider whether some stationery can be totally interchangeable between the libraries. A number of items could fall into this category. Stationery which is used in the library only has no need to have the library's address printed on it – for example enrolment cards, reservation cards perhaps, and thus one design can be used in all branches. Items of stationery which are sent out to the public need to carry the address of the library. Decide if this needs to be printed on or whether a single rubber stamp would be adequate. If the address has to be printed on this will mean a separate piece of artwork and more and shorter print runs. If the rubber stamp solution is acceptable then economy can be achieved by one piece of artwork and one long print run.

Stationery can also provide economies by the use of multiple-message forms – for example reservation cards. All the common messages that are sent out to readers should be analysed and a series of post-cards eoncompassing these can be designed. The use of computerised systems reduces the need for the pre-printing of some of these messages since they will be produced by the machine on demand. It is possible to have such computer-produced messages put onto cards pre-printed with the library logo. The extra work of this may be worth it to produce a more important looking result. Postcards to users telling them that reserved books are available or that items are overdue are also statements in the library's corporate identity programme. They advertise the library and its services to the public and it is worthwhile making an effort with them.

Letterheads and compliment slips play a major part in spreading the identity of the library. The use of the library logo and the layout of letters etc are all valuable in creating a favourable impression. Address labels for parcels and packets make even re-used "Jiffy bags" look respectable and important. Labels should incorporate the library logo so that they can be returned in the event on non-delivery, and also to advertise the library. Books lent on interlibrary loan should include a gummed address label for the return of the loan. Other stationery associated with interlibrary loans are request cards for users to fill in and a bookmark to tell the reader that the item has been borrowed from another library. This latter also explains the special loan to the user and obviates the need for library staff to tell the user each time.

Enrolment forms and reader tickets can usually be one design for the whole library system. If it is necessary to indicate which libraries the reader may use this can be done by adding some form of code to the ticket which can be marked by library staff or with a rubber stamp.

Having produced a comprehensive design programme for the library it is necessary to prevent it being sabotaged! It is impossible to provide notices for every occasion and possibility and there is a danger that temporary notices will be messy and scruffy. At the same time it would obviously be uneconomical to produce a specific printed notice for each of these short term needs. Some can be predicted however and it is worth producing some to meet these eventualities. Each branch of the library should have at least one notice which says "Out of order" or "Machine not working – Technician notified" to deal with equipment breakdown, particularly necessary when there is a photocopier on the premises!

For the unpredictable crisis however or to deal with temporary changes etc in the library it is useful to provide notice blanks with the library logo on. These can be used as temporary notices and even when handwritten have a professional and official look which no scribbled piece of paper can ever have. The production of two formats, in A4 size, one landscape, one portrait, will cope with almost every possible need. All staff should be given instructions on the use of these and stocks should be kept in every service point. The use of other temporary notices should be severely castigated. If the library

**WESTBRIDGE
UNIVERSITY
LIBRARY**

PSALTER LANE SITE
Psalter Lane

Telephone
56101
Ext. 30

Please see no.

1. Please return or renew.

2. Requested by another reader. Please return.

3. Item available in Short Loan Collection.

4. Please collect by

---

**WESTBRIDGE
UNIVERSITY
LIBRARY**

PSALTER LANE SITE
Psalter Lane

Telephone
56101
Ext. 30

We have been unable to trace a copy
of this item so far. Please see no.

1. Do you still require this item?

2. Do you wish us to apply to another library?

3. Do you wish us to apply abroad? This will
   entail some delay.

4. Please supply a photocopy of your source
   of reference.

**From:**

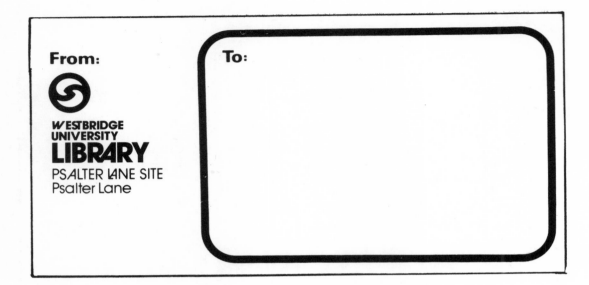

**WESTBRIDGE
UNIVERSITY
LIBRARY**
PSALTER LANE SITE
Psalter Lane

**To:**

---

**To: WESTBRIDGE
UNIVERSITY
LIBRARY**
PSALTER LANE SITE
Psalter Lane

# This item

does not belong to us; it has been kindly lent by another library.

Will you please, therefore, take particular care to return it to this library not later than

Should you wish to retain the item for a further period, please apply to the library at least two clear days before the date given above.

---

Please note that failure to comply with the above conditions may make it difficult to secure a similar privilege for you in the future.

---

**WESTBRIDGE UNIVERSITY LIBRARY**

Enrolment form

| | |
|---|---|
| Surname | |
| Forenames | |
| Termtime address | |
| Home address (if different from above) | |
| Course | Department |
| Details of employer if short course/conference member | |
| Signature | Date |

Please tick

Full time student
Part time student
Staff
Other

Please circle year of course

1 2 3 4 5

For Library Staff use

---

**WESTBRIDGE UNIVERSITY LIBRARY** 1982·83 PL CC WW

This card must be produced each time a book is borrowed.

Loss of this card must be reported to the Library immediately.

Signature

# WESTBRIDGE
# UNIVERSITY
# LIBRARY

CLOSED
DUE TO
ILLNESS

REOPEN 2pm

has a programme of exhibitions or concerts a special series of blank posters can be printed which will then be overprinted with the detail of each event. This gives a coordinated look to the programme and identifies it as being in the library. It is economical too in that posters do not have to be individually designed for each event in the programme once the basic design and layout has been decided.

Cataloguing stationery will vary, depending on the system used, with on-line cataloguing being most economical, in terms of printed stationery at least. Systems which use forms to be completed by the cataloguer for later input into machine readable form or catalogue card production by typists are obviously paper-intensive. The life of the form is relatively short and it will be discarded after the data is put into a different format. The essential here is cheapness of production. There is no sense in using high-quality paper. The form is for internal use only so the minimum quality of production should be sought compatible with care of use by the staff. Nevertheless the quality of *design* should not be lowered, and the criteria in the indentity manual should apply even to these cheaply-produced sheets.

Book order forms should be produced to a high standard. Multi-part forms using NCR paper will produce copies for a variety of files in the ordering system. Even a computerised system will probably need some form of paper order to go to some of the booksellers at least and there will always be a need for some manual orders, perhaps to small specialist booksellers or publishers, second-hand dealers, or sources which are not really geared up to the sale of books or a.v. materials to libraries, such as the purchase of exhibition catalogues from art galleries and museums.

Book stationery should be coordinated throughout the system. Categories of books may be differentiated by coloured date labels, or all may be white overstamped as appropriate. The latter method is obviously more economical. Colour coding to indicate loan categories can also be used on spine labels.

Any change in book stationery will take a long time to work through the stock and older little-used material will harbour ancient stationery which may almost be of historical interest! The introduction of the corporate identity programme is an opportunity to review the way that the book stock is labelled. Much will depend on the issue system but there are always economies possible – for example there is no need to print lines on a date label if staff are trained to stamp the return date in columns. The use of bar-code labels for computerised issue systems means that a possession stamp could be incorporated on this stick-on label, allowing the use of a plain gummed date label. Book pockets for a Browne issue system are more effectively made by folded date/possession labels rather than sticking in extra manila pockets. Wherever possible the labelling and possession stamping of material should be done by booksellers if they are able to do it as it frees library staff from this chore.

The sizes of stationery should be limited, preferably to standard sizes in the A range since this will allow more economical printing. Consideration has to be given to existing drawers and storage units however and most libraries will have plenty of drawers suitable for 5" x 3" cards. This factor will outweigh the additional slight costs caused by waste card in the printing process. There may be problems getting the data required onto 5" x 3" cards – A6 size might be better.

The language of library stationery and leaflets should be very carefully thought out. There has been considerable publicity about the redesign of government forms and information leaflets. Librarians should bear these lessons in mind when writing their own forms for public use. Avoid librarianship jargon completely. This is likely to be the most pernicious fault as it can be difficult to detect; librarians often forget that the public will not appreciate what their terminology means. Consider too the level of the audience. The language applicable to undergraduates will be different from that suitable for children. Do not overload the information in each sentence. Keep the sentences and paragraphs short and use different weights of type if possible, or spacing of lines to achieve emphasis of the important elements.

Some forms which will be used as a basis for keypunching often require the users to write each letter in a separate box. Despite the prevalence of the practice most members of the public find it awkward to fill in such forms and in fact the results are often full of faults as far as the keyboard operators are concerned. It is probably better to ask people to fill in the form legibly in capital letters without providing the boxes except when asking them to provide certain types of information, for example a course code in an academic library, where the provision of boxes ensures that the correct number of digits is put in.

Coloured paper and card can be used for stationery or in other aspects of the corporate identity programme. Different colours can be used for different branches or stationery for particular functional areas of the library can be differentiated by colours.

The range of stationery necessary will vary from library system to library system but as with the guiding there are some items which could be designed for use in many systems. A number of these are included at the end of the book.

The design of any individual form can be made easier by the following considerations:

1 Are there any size parameters – eg what storage is already available: the form must fit into particular envelopes etc?
2 What information needs to be on the form? List these.
3 Consider if any of these items of information must go in a particular place on the form, eg. if it is being used for filing it should be at the top, signature and date normally go at the bottom etc.
4 Consider how much space each element of information will need.
5 Arrange all the elements into a logical order, keeping together any "For Staff use" parts.
6 Fit this logical order into the space available. Areas for staff use can be squeezed into the right hand side.

**WESTBRIDGE UNIVERSITY**
**LIBRARY** Pond Street Site
enrolment form

Please use Block Capitals

Mr/Mrs/Miss/Ms    Initials

8                                 12

Surname

15

dept. and site

8

28

Home Address

8

28

48

Termtime Address (students)

Please tick    Full time student ☐    Staff ☐
               Part time student ☐    Misc ☐

**I undertake to obey library rules and will be held responsible for damage to or loss of library property while in my charge.**

Signature _____ Date _____

**Students only:**

Year of course (please ring)  1st/2nd/3rd/4th

Calendar year
course ends        1  9              Course _____

---

**For Library use only**

Borrower No                              Usage count:

2

Form punched (init.) _____

**Lost Cards**

1 Signature of borrower _____

Date _____

New no

Old no. restricted(init.) _____

New details punched(init.) _____

2 Signature of borrower _____

Date _____

New no

Old no. restricted(init.) _____

New details punched(init.) _____

Continue in same way overleaf  if
necessary.

Dept and Course           End year        **Delete**

69                        74               78

7    If this is unsuccessful look again at how much space is available. If necessary rethink both space and information.

The main points to consider in stationery design are

1    Stationery design often carries the corporate identity programme outside the library, so should be given as much consideration as other aspects of the programme.
2    Economy of production by standardisation of forms, cards, etc.
3    Language and information should be appropriate to the audience.
4    Do not allow staff to stick up temporary notices except on official blanks.

# 12. Publishing for Sale

In addition to providing information for their users many libraries also produce materials for sale to the public. The range of such potential saleable items is endless, but is particularly strong in the field of local history. Reproductions of old maps, other documents (prints and photographs) from the library's collection, will usually find a ready market. Post cards of old street scenes for example are particularly popular. In addition to the straight reprinting of older material it is possible to use the originals in new formats. Old prints can be used on greetings cards or mugs for example. All such printing can be done under the direction of the librarian – it is similar to the production of the stationery and publications being printed for the Library's own use. The only difference here is that they are for sale, and it is important to build in data on the costs of production so that the items will be correctly priced.

The reprinting of most substantial items however is not something that can be undertaken lightly. If a complete book is to be reprinted it is best to deal with a specialist firm. The costs involved in commercial publishing and the equipment needed for book production make this essential. Before such an undertaking is commenced it is necessary to do some basic market research into possible sales. The publisher will probably quote for a minimum number of copies, and it is not economic to have large stocks of a book not selling. Reasonable expectation of sales should cover the actual costs of printing, binding etc, with additional sales being profit. It may be possible to obtain advance subscription to a forthcoming reprint of a book of great local interest in which case the sales of a certain number of copies at least are guaranteed, reducing the risk of catastrophe. Other factors to be considered are the retail price of the book, what discount will be offered for bulk purchase etc.

Local booksellers will expect the usual trade discount if they are to stock the library's book. Since such outlets will increase the potential market for the book it is essential to build in allowances for trade discounts in the final price. Check with the treasurer's or finance department of the parent institution what procedures will need to be set up to deal with income from the sale of books and other publications. Ensure that where appropriate ISBNs and ISSNs are assigned. Librarians at least ought to make sure that these are right. Once a book has been decided on for reprinting it is necessary to plan a strategy for publicity. Advance notice in the form of a press release or similar sheet should be sent to local papers, booksellers, societies and associations who might be interested in it. Posters can be produced using the artwork for the front cover of the book which can then be displayed in all the library's service points and anywhere else that can be persuaded to display them. Smaller advertising leaflets, A5 size or smaller, can be produced for library users to take, or bookmarks can be used to advertise the forthcoming work.

The actual publication of the book may be the occasion for some form of launch party, or it may simply appear on sale. Review copies should be sent to appropriate papers and journals. Copies of the actual book should be available at all service points and staff should be instructed on any special details about the money taken in sales eg. "Cash from books is to be kept separate from fines".

A similar procedure will need to be followed if the book is not a straight reprint of an old book but specially commissioned. In this case however the librarian needs to keep an even closer eye on what is being done. The new artwork for covers, title page etc should be checked to ensure that it meets the library's identity standards. Details of royalties if any, should be clarified and some form of contract drawn up between the library and the author. In both cases the librarian should make sure that the book is deposited at the British Library and gets into BNB, *British Books in Print* etc. Its appearance in these bibliographies is a useful source of sales.

## SALES

In addition to books, pamphlets, pictures and postcards, other materials for sale can include carrier bags, car stickers, badges, balloons, mugs and other souvenirs. Such promotional material can be obtained from specialist suppliers/printers and should be priced so that the library makes a profit on each item. If the library holds significant runs of old periodicals or a collection of rare books it may be possible to persuade a microfilm publisher to reprint these on fiche or microfilm. The amount of income to the library from the sale of these will normally only be a reproduction fee or possibly some small royalty on each sale. Nevertheless, there is prestige attached to the use of a library's materials in such a publishing programme which may be good for the library's identity. The library could also act as its own publisher of microfilms or a.v. material for books.

A particular category of sale is to other libraries. Such material might be periodical lists, current awareness publications etc. Any data that can be stored in a computerised file can be produced on microfiche at fairly low cost.

Indexes to a local history collection, periodical lists etc are all possible sources of revenue on fiche. Fiche can also be produced by photographic processes, to reproduce a picture collection for example, but the costs involved in this are far greater. If the library is producing a copy for itself however to record holdings it is a relatively cheap process to duplicate the fiche. Sales could then be used to offset some of the costs of the master production. The market for sales to libraries however is likely to be relatively limited unless the material has a very wide usage. Often it will be local or specific subject interest.

Where the library charges subscriptions to a service, such as a record or video library, it would be possible to sell tokens towards the cost of such services. With an attractively designed greetings card these might be particularly popular at Christmas. The cost of producing the card would have to be borne by the library but these could be a gain in subscription which would offset the extra printing cost.

Publishing for sale is an area which will undoubtedly become more important as the library seeks to generate income. The librarian should consider the following points before embarking on this:

1  What material is available which could be used to raise money?
2  Are there any copyright restrictions in force on this material?
3  Costs of production, and costs of wholesale and retail sales.
4  Staff time involved in sales.
5  Financial procedures.
6  Is there a market for the sale of items to the users?
7  Are there other markets the library could tap – other libraries etc?
8  Should one member of staff be given the overall responsibility for this aspect of the library's activities?

# 13. Dealing with the Professional

When dealing with other professionals such as designers, printers, photographers etc it is important for the librarian to realise that they are experts in their field and to treat them with the respect that they deserve. Remember however that they are not librarians and probably have little knowledge of what libraries are about beyond a superficial level. It is necessary therefore to provide all such outside professionals with some form of brief or instructions so that they carry out their work to the librarian's satisfaction and so that all sides are agreed as to what they are trying to achieve.

## BRIEFING

Explain in detail, in clear unambiguous language what the job entails. "Print 400 leaflets" is not a very helpful brief to a printer. Better would be something like: "Print 400 leaflets, A5 size, black ink on buff 80gm paper, printed both sides – artwork enclosed".

For a designer it is important to explain what the finished result is to achieve; "Construct a free-standing plan of the Library's lower floor which can be sited near the stairs to orientate users after coming downstairs".

Include any parameters of size, colour, costs etc if appropriate: "The plan should be A2 size, with colour coding matching the guiding of the lower floor – details enclosed".
"Please submit a written estimate of costs before commencing work".

Instructions as to delivery or collection and any deadlines should also be included to avoid possible recriminations at a later date:
"The printed work to be collected by Mr Kirby on Friday 6th April. Please telephone if this deadline cannot be met".
"Please deliver finished signs to Jane Farrell in the Library. Invoices should be sent to the Library Secretary at . . .".

Make a note of dates of sending artwork to printers etc so that you have a record of what is where in the production schedule. It is always helpful to be able to answer a query about some publication's progress with an answer such as "It went to the printers last Tuesday, and it should be delivered by the end of the week". At the very least this gives an air of efficiency on the part of the librarian!

# PRODUCTION CHECKLIST

TITLE

LIBRARIAN RESPONSIBLE

TEXT     Draft          Final          Typed/Typeset

ARTWORK                    Approved

ESTIMATE                   FINAL COST

PRINTER                    DATE SENT

FORMAT                     QUANTITY

MATERIALS                  COLOUR

INK COLOUR

WANTED BY

DELIVER TO

INVOICE TO

ORDER NO                   INVOICE NO

NOTES

# TALKING TO THE PROFESSIONALS

When dealing with professionals it can be helpful for the librarian to provide a sample or a sketch of what he wants. Many of these professionals will be more used to dealing in visual terms than verbal instructions and a quick drawing is often easier to understand than a paragraph of words. But do not take over the design process. They are experts in fields other than librarianship. If you could do their job as well as being a librarian there would be no need to go to them in the first place. Do not try to tell them their job; do make use of their expertise. In most cases they will be delighted to explain the complexities of their skill to you. Do not be afraid to admit your ignorance. There is no point bluffing and pretending knowledge you do not have. If found out you will lose their respect. Ask their advice and discuss with them what you want to achieve and the best means to achieve it.

On the other hand do not be fobbed off with something you do not want or that is inappropriate to the library's needs. Glossy brochures may be suitable for the advertising industry but are probably not appropriate as handouts to hundreds of undergraduate students. In particular be sure to explain the identity programme, in detail. If the logo must appear in a particular place, then ensure that the designer is aware of this and insist that he carry out the work within the specifications to the manual.

# FINDING THE PROFESSIONALS

This will depend on the circumstances of each library. If the policy of the institution is to use its own print unit then the Librarian's work ends there. If there is no policy, or no print unit in-house, the Librarian should seek outside. Trade directories, phone books etc are useful sources of information. Word-of-mouth information is often better. A recommendation to a good printer from a respected source is worth following up. Printing in particular is a highly competitive business so the Librarian should obtain quotes from at least two printers for different types of job. Consider delivery times, general willingness to be helpful, proximity to the library etc in addition to the financial costs. It can be particularly useful to have a printer just round the corner – it is much easier to confront him about problems in person rather than shout down a telephone! Delivery too is likely to be quicker.

Check the printer's own parameters. What size paper can he handle? Colour printing? Folding, collating, stapling? Other binding options for booklets? Look at samples of other work done by the printer – be very wary if he is reluctant to show you some.

Many 'fast printers' and 'copyshops' can only do a limited range of printing, but they may be willing, as will a larger printer, to do artwork and graphic design for the library. Check the costs. Weigh up the quality of the finished product compared with what can be done at lower cost within the library. It may be worth paying the extra to get a highly professional looking result. Ensure that the professionals and the Librarian are in agreement about payment, whether cash with order, on collection, by invoice etc. The Librarian should be clear in his own mind about any internal ramifications relating to ordering and should ensure that there are no hold-ups in the Accounts Department in the payment of invoices. Remember that many of the professionals that the library will be dealing with are not cushioned by being part of a large institution and that they rely for their existence on a reasonable cash-flow. Late payment of a local printer by an institution can ruin the relationship that the Librarian has worked to develop. It is also embarrassing, time-wasting and occasionally unpleasant for both sides to get into this situation. The Librarian therefore should do everything to avoid it happening.

Other sources of information about the professionals include trade exhibitions, catalogues, periodicals, advertisements etc. The Librarian should assemble as much ephemera as possible that might be useful in finding either services or products of use in the indentity programme. In addition he should keep his eyes open when away from the library for ideas and items that could be used in a library context. For example leaflet dispensers in the hotel foyer could be useful in the library too, so check who makes them; the sign system in that store might have a use in the library, make a note of the design.

Finally beware of library suppliers. Use them if their products seem suited to the library, but it is worth checking another supplier before ordering. Often the library could buy the identical product cheaper elsewhere.

The librarian should take note of the following points when dealing with the professionals:

1    Provide a detailed brief and instructions.
2    Shop around for the best deal.
3    Do not be fobbed off with something the library does not want.
4    Do not tell them how to do their jobs. Use their expertise to the library's advantage.

# Glossary

This glossary contains some terms which may be unfamiliar to librarians who have not worked in this area before.

**'A' RANGE OF PAPER SIZES**: Following the recommendations of the International Organization for Standardization a series of paper sizes has been introduced called the 'A' series. The basis of the series is the proportion of one side of the sheet to the other of $1 : \sqrt{2}$. The actual sizes of the sheets are:

| | | |
|---|---|---|
| A0 | 841mm x 1189mm | 33.11in x 46.81in |
| A1 | 594mm x 841mm | 23.39in x 33.11in |
| A2 | 420mm x 594mm | 16.54in x 23.39in |
| A3 | 297mm x 420mm | 11.69in x 16.54in |
| A4 | 210mm x 297mm | 8.27in x 11.69in |
| A5 | 148mm x 210mm | 5.83in x 8.27in |
| A6 | 105mm x 148mm | 4.13in x 5.83in |
| A7 | 74mm x 105mm | 2.91in x 4.13in |

**ARTWORK**: Artwork is the black and white original that goes to the printer from which he makes the printing-plate. If more than one colour is to be printed a separate piece of artwork must be prepared for each colour.

**CAKE PLAN**: A cake plan is a representation of a vertical slice of a building giving details of what is available on each level. It thus looks like a slice of sponge cake, filled with cream and jam.

**CORPORATE IDENTITY**: This is the public face of the organisation, created by a variety of means including the use of standardised lettering, uniform appearance of buildings, stationery etc.

**END GUIDES**: These are guides at the ends of units of shelving, indicating what is on either side of the bay.

**GRID**: The layout grid is an aid to preparation of artwork, ensuring a consistent appearance to a range of publications, the pages in a book etc., without the need to remeasure the page each time. It defines the areas of particular parts of the page, eg text area, logo, position of page numbers etc.

**IDENTITY & IMAGE**: Throughout this book the following definitions have been used for Identity and Image: Identity is a consciously sought appearance, deliberately contrived to create a particular impression; Image is the randomly achieved appearance in the mind of the library user. The two are not incompatible; the librarian could seek an identity for the library of calm efficiency, but the users could gain an image of harassed chaos. The aim of the identity programme described in the book is to bring these two elements closer together.

**LAYOUT GRID**: see GRID.

**LOGO**: The logo is the stylised form of the organisation's name, either in a symbol or typographical form, or both. The logo is one of the most common elements of the corporate identity.

**NCR PAPER**: No Carbon Required Paper is used in multipart forms to produce information on each sheet from the writing on the top copy. Although convenient it is relatively expensive and the results are variable, particularly from handwriting.

**PASTE-UP**: This is the technique which can be used to produce artwork. It consists of sticking the various elements of the artwork onto a white sheet of paper or card. The edges of the paper do not show when the printing-plate is made.

**PICTOGRAM**: A standardised picture or symbol for certain services or prohibitions, eg No Smoking, Fire Extinguisher etc. Unfortunately these standardised signs are not as standard as they might be, and there can be confusion as to the meaning of some pictograms. If in doubt use the pictogram plus a verbal equivalent.

**SHELF GUIDES**: These are guide strips placed on the actual shelf to which they refer. Only useful for stock which does not get moved around or if they are moved with the books.

**SLAT GUIDING**: A system of guiding using slats, each panel containing one message. The advantage is that it is a flexible system, slats being added or removed as appropriate when the library changes without the need to redesign all the sign each time.

**TIER GUIDES**: These are guide strips above a tier of shelves. Usually of a general subject guide to the books in that tier.

# Bibliography

The highly selective bibliography below includes only items which I have found useful or interesting, but the literature relating to this subject is enormous and there are many other valuable works available.

The most fruitful sources of ideas on creating the library identity however come not from books but from looking at how other organisations cope with problems and then translating these concepts into a library environment.

*ASLIB Proceedings*, October 1981, Vol 33 No 10. Reports a one day conference relating to library publicity and identity.

BALLINGER, Raymond A. *Layout and graphic design*. Van Nostrand Reinhold, 1980.

BERRYMAN, Gregg. *Notes on graphic design and visual communication*. Kaufman, 1980.

BOOTH-CLIBBORN, Edward & BARONI, Daniele. *The language of graphics*. Thames & Hudson, 1980.

BRITISH COUNCIL. Social communication; public information graphics in Britain. British Council, 1979.

BROEKHUIZEN, R. *Graphic communications*. McKnight, 1979.

CARTER, D. *Corporate identity manuals*. Century communications, 1976.

DALLEY, Terence. *Complete guide to illustration and design*. Phaidon, 1980.

DAVIS, Alec. *Graphics; design to production*. Faber, 1973.

DEMONEY, J. & MEYER, S. *Paste-ups and mechanicals*. Watson-Guptill, 1982.

GARLAND, Ken. Graphics handbook. Studio Vista, 1966.

GOODCHILD, John & HENKIN, Bill. *By design; a graphics source-book of materials, equipment and services*. Quick Fox, 1980.

GRAY, Bill. *Studio tips for artists and graphic designers*. Van Nostrand 1976, and *More studio tips*, VNR, 1978.

HARESNAPE, Brian. *British Rail, 1948–1978; a journey by design*. Ian Allan, 1979.

HURLBUT, Allen. *Publication design*. Van Nostrand Reinhold, 1976.

McLENDON, C. *Signage; graphic communications in the built world*. McGraw-Hill, 1982.

OLINS, Wally. *The corporate personality*. Design Council, 1978.

PORTER, Tom & GREENSTREET, Bob. *Manual of graphic techniques for architects, graphic designers and artists*. Astragal, 1980.

REYNOLDS, Linda & BARRETT, Stephen. *Signs and guiding for libraries*. Bingley, 1980.

SUTTER, Jan. *Slinging ink; a practical guide to producing booklets, newspapers and ephemeral publications*. Kaufman, 1982.

TREWEEK, C. & ZEILLYN, J. *The alternative printing handbook*. Penguin, 1983.

VAN UCHELEN, Rod. *Paste-up; production techniques and new applications*.

In addition to the above books there are a number of journals on graphics, though many of them are rather specialised. The ones below are those I found useful as an untrained designer!

*Campaign* The magazine of the advertising industry in the UK. Useful for current-awareness on how commerce is promoting itself. Even more useful as a source of ideas and suppliers for printers, promotional services etc.

*Design* Probably the best general design journal, full of interesting new developments in many fields.

*Graphics World* A practical graphics journal, understandable even to the librarian with limited expertise.

*Information Design Journal* Extremely useful information on all aspects of written and visual communication, including the design of forms, signs, layout etc.

*Infuse* and the *LIMB Index*. Both published from Loughborough University. Specific current-awareness on research and practice in libraries.

# INDEX